THE GEOGRAPHY
OF FRONTIERS AND BOUNDARIES

The Geography
of Frontiers and Boundaries

J. R. V. PRESCOTT

Senior Lecturer in Geography
University of Melbourne

ALDINE PUBLISHING COMPANY
CHICAGO

First published 1965 by
ALDINE PUBLISHING COMPANY
320 West Adams Street
Chicago, Illinois 60606
and
Hutchinson & Co. Ltd., London

Library of Congress Catalog Card Number 65-23531

Second printing 1967

Printed in the United States of America

Contents

Maps

Preface

I would like to thank Professor W. G. East for his initial suggestion that I should write this book and for his many helpful comments on the material used. I am also grateful to Professor O. H. K. Spate, Professor S. B. Jones and Professor R. Hartshorne for helpful suggestions about various sections of the work; to the reference staff of the Baillieu Library in the University of Melbourne for their patient collection of references from many Australian and Overseas sources; and to my wife for preparing the index.

J. R. V. PRESCOTT

1

Concepts and terminology

Le caractère marquant de la notion de frontière est son
universalité d'acception. De l'homme de rue ou du paysan
jusqu'au politique et au savant, elle est susceptible, selon
les catégories et les classes, de rencontrer les interprétations
les plus diverses. (Lapradelle, 1928, p. 9)

Le sujet (les frontières), avouons-le, est dangereux pour
un savant, car il est tout pénétré de passions politiques,
tout encombrés d'arrière-pensées. Les gens ont trop
d'intérêts en jeu, quand ils parlent de frontières, pour en
parler de sang-froid: le malentendu est permanent!
(Siegfried, writing in Ancel, 1938, p. vii)

It is impossible to study boundaries and frontiers without being
continually aware of the points made by these distinguished authors.
First, there is the challenge of studying a subject which has general
appeal, and which is of crucial importance in the field of political
geography and international relations. The second point arises from
the first and concerns the need to clear the mind of subjective views
which will influence the selection of facts and presentation of cases.
The danger of subjectivity is probably greater in political geography
than in any other branch of the subject. Failure to maintain objec-
tivity would be academically embarrassing to a geomorphologist or
historical geographer, and would detract from the value of his
completed work, but the present century has seen how subjective
studies in political geography can be perverted to political arguments which can have far-reaching consequences. Every effort has
been made to preserve the present study from prejudice, and the
author is grateful that it is made at a time when the passions

generated by the second world war have largely disappeared and when there is no threatening shadow of further world conflicts. This advantage was denied to such authors as Holdich, Haushofer and Ancel.

A comprehensive review of the literature in the field of boundary and frontier studies is not possible in the space available, and it has been decided to review the works of ten authors who have written generally on this subject and span the period 1895–1957. This historical review will be followed by a summary of the main concepts agreed by the authors, an outline of the terminology used in this book, and an indication of the general plan of the remaining chapters.

Ratzel's concept of boundaries followed logically from his view of the state as a living organism. The boundary was the skin of the living state and like the epidermis of animals and plants it provided defence and allowed exchange to occur. This fundamental belief provided the point from which Ratzel sought to define the character of boundaries and the way in which they altered.

First, Ratzel maintained that the boundary was an abstraction and that the border area (*Grenzraum*) was the reality.

> Der Grenzraum ist das Wirkliche, die Grenzlinie die Abstraktion
> davon.   (Ratzel, 1895, p. 538)

According to Ratzel the border consisted of three zones, two of which were the periphery of the adjoining states, and the third a central zone where there was a mingling of the two states. This was a concept accepted and developed by Lapradelle when he considered boundaries in relation to international law.

In developing the same theme Ratzel maintained that it was unrealistic to attempt to dissect the boundary from the state for individual study. Again and again it was stressed that the fringes of the state were an integral part of the whole and that it was unrealistic to talk of the greater importance of the centre (Ratzel, 1895, pp. 605–6, and p. 614 ff). This view underlay the second point which was that boundaries were a factor influencing state power and a measure of state power.

In den Grenzen liegt ein guter Teil der Gewichte des politischen
Gleichgewichts.   (Ratzel, 1895, p. 584)

Wir haben gesehen, wie Wachstum und Rückgang des Gebietes nicht
bloss in der Gestalt und den Schutzvorrichtungen der Grenze Ausdruck
finden, sondern sich auch gleichsam darin vorbereiten und ankündigen.
                                                   (Ratzel, 1895, p. 605)

This view that the boundary-zone was the area within which growth
and decline of the state were organized and evidenced was responsible for the emphasis given to territorial adjustment by the geopoliticians thirty years later, and was the precise view attacked
consistently, if unsuccessfully, by Ancel. For Ratzel the strongest
states showed close ties between the border and state core. Any
tendency for the connexions to be weakened would weaken the
state and result in the loss of the border through its assertion of
independence or its incorporation within a neighbouring state. The
capacity of the boundary to change was a third important point.
Ratzel noted that the boundaries of larger states would often
absorb the territories of smaller adjacent states and that in all
cases a state would strive for the best possible boundary, which was
usually the shortest (Ratzel, 1895, pp. 555 and 557). The state
should also seek to establish strong military boundaries which
would involve controlling the trans-mountain slopes and the further
banks of rivers. This concern with strong strategic boundaries was
later echoed by Lord Curzon (1907) and Holdich (1916). Ratzel's
advocacy of boundaries founded on physical features was not
unqualified. He pointed out that not all natural boundaries were
good boundaries and indicated clearly that the quality of the
population, the available resources, and the prevailing political
situation were also factors which had to be considered (pp. 585–6).
Ratzel was convinced that the boundary would change as the
relationship between the states altered, and also pointed out that
the functions applied at boundaries would alter as federations of
states were formed. He used the formation of Germany as an
example of this and went on to point out the corollary that if
boundaries were reduced in status then they might continue to
demarcate variations in the landscape which their existence had

fostered. These were the relict boundaries which Hartshorne identified in 1936.

The imperfections of Ratzel's organic theories of the state have been exposed by many writers, yet surprisingly not all his concepts about boundaries have foundered. This is probably because Ratzel tried to establish laws about boundary development and behaviour. The futility of this work has been demonstrated by Jones (1945) who correctly regards each boundary as unique. However, Ratzel's so-called laws would undoubtedly apply to certain boundaries.

> Dem allgemeinen Gesetz des Wachstumes der geschichtlichen Räume Folgend, nehmen die Grenzen der grösseren Gebiete die Grenzen der kleineren in sich auf.   (Ratzel, 1895, p. 555)

> Das Gesetz der Entwicklung der Grenzen kann als Streben nach Vereinfachung bezeichnet werden, und diese Vereinfachung schliesst die Verkürzung in sich.   (Ratzel, 1895, p. 557)

Cases can be discovered which fit these patterns of development but there will be as many or more exceptions. Ratzel has been criticized for providing the concepts which assisted the development of theories of *Geopolitik*, and because he was too deterministic in according the major role to physical factors of geography. These criticisms are less applicable to his theories about boundaries than his overall theories about states. When his work became better known in the post-World War I period, the subject would have advanced more quickly if writers had attempted to build on the sound parts of his structure instead of concentrating on those which were transparently faulty. The continued criticism of the concept of natural and artificial boundaries was not justified in view of the qualifications which Ratzel made about the merit of natural boundaries, in respect of the quality of the population and the nature of political circumstances.

Lord Curzon (1907) brought his experience as a diplomat and administrator to bear in preparing the Romanes lecture. His interest in boundaries lay in their importance in international relations, and his lecture was delivered close to the end of one of the most intensive periods of boundary-construction the European Powers had ever known. He was aware of this and expected that the following period would be calmer with disputes being settled by international law rather than military forays. The main part of his lecture examined the strength and weakness of the two main types of boundaries – natural and artificial. By these terms Curzon referred to boundaries which were dependent upon, or independent of, physical features of the Earth's surface. He considered this classification to enjoy general recognition and possess the most scientific character. These were terms which were used by Holdich but which other writers attacked on the logical grounds that all boundaries were artificial, and that the implication of the expression 'natural' was that such boundaries were intrinsically more appropriate than boundaries not based on the physical landscape. The point is worth making that Lord Curzon's view was that boundaries located within some physical feature such as a mountain range or desert were superior to other kinds because they offered better opportunities for defence. None of Lord Curzon's critics seems to have given him credit for distinguishing clearly between 'natural boundaries' which were based on some physical feature and a 'class of so-called Natural Frontiers . . . namely those which are claimed by nations as natural on grounds of ambition, or expediency, or more often sentiment. The attempt to realize Frontiers of this type has been responsible for many of the wars, and some of the most tragical vicissitudes in history' (Curzon, 1907, p. 54). In other words, Lord Curzon knew exactly what he meant and there was no confusion in his mind.

One of the least satisfactory features of the essay was the use of 'frontier' and 'boundary' as interchangeable terms, but since Boggs in 1940 followed the same rule, although he noted the real difference, one cannot criticize Curzon too much. His essay contained several points, which were further developed by later writers. He carefully followed Macmahon in distinguishing between the demarcation and delimitation of boundaries, and put forward three ideas which were later used by others. First, artificial frontiers were classified into three groups: astronomical, mathematical and referential. The astronomical boundaries followed a parallel of latitude or a meridian; the mathematical boundaries connected two specified points; and the referential boundaries were defined with regard to some point or points and included arcs of circles and straight lines. This classification was later used by Fawcett and Lapradelle. Second, Curzon briefly mentioned the idea of distinguishing between frontiers of separation and contact, which was later developed by Fawcett and East and is used in this book. Lastly, in the conclusion, Curzon noted that it was important to study the effects of the boundaries upon fortifications which are aspects of border landscapes, and to revalue continually the suitability of boundaries in the light of technical advances, especially of those in the conduct of warfare. This was an early hint which was not accepted by geographers for a considerable period.

Colonel Sir T. H. Holdich based his study of boundaries in 1916 on his practical experience of many boundary commissions. He deplored the lack of experience on the part of some earlier authors and singled out the idealistic views of Lyde for particularly unfavourable comment. Lyde (1915) had suggested in his book, which was subtitled *An aspiration for Europe*, that boundaries should be drawn to give states maximum ethnic homogeneity, and through areas where population would meet and, he hoped, mingle. Lyde also suggested that before any area was transferred to another state the ability of the recipient to assimililate the new population should be considered. Holdich criticized the first two arguments. His experience had taught him that boundaries should be strong.

> Boundaries must be barriers – if not geographical and natural they must be artificial and strong as military device can make them.
>
> (Holdich, 1916, p. 46)

He criticized those states in central Europe which were seeking extended ethnographic boundaries rather than selecting strong strategic boundaries which would leave some minorities outside, but which would offer greater security to the people within the state. Following Lord Curzon, Holdich used the terms 'frontier' and 'boundary' as synonyms, but he did draw attention to the difference between them.

> Nature knows no boundary line. Nature has her frontiers truly, but lines, especially straight lines, are abhorrent to her.
>
> (Holdich, 1916, p. 2)

Later Holdich distinguished between 'natural frontiers' and 'artificial boundaries', thereby indicating an awareness of the difference which subsequent critics have not always granted. The advantages and disadvantages of the two main categories of divides were examined, in terms of defence and ease of demarcation. This last aspect was important to Holdich and it is characteristic of the man that he thought that

> the escort difficulty is perhaps the most important consideration of any in the arrangements for the successful conduct of the working party.
> (Holdich, 1916, p. 213)

Holdich wrote his book at the time when the military techniques being displayed in Europe called for strong defensive positions, regularly buttressed with fortresses. He believed this would remain the general pattern and was thus encouraged in his advocacy of strong boundaries.

The book contains a rich store of anecdotes and serves to underline the fact that boundary-making is a practical art. His examples provide the raw material for generalizations but remind the student that the abstractions should not be carried too far. This is a point which was most forcibly made by Jones (1945) nearly thirty years later.

Fawcett (1918) was primarily concerned with the geographical facts of frontiers and draws a clear distinction between their zonal characteristics and the linear nature of boundaries. There is an excellent chapter on the nature of frontiers at the physical, cultural and political levels. He concludes that frontiers are distinct regions of transition; while it is admitted that all regions are transitional, it is only when the transitional feature is the dominant characteristic that the region is a true frontier. Fawcett attacks the division of frontiers into natural and artificial categories. He does so in rather a curious way for, while he notes that the division is based upon the degree of association with physical features, he attacks the terms since the evolution of all kinds of boundaries is natural. Fawcett in fact tended to perpetuate the term 'artificial' in developing Curzon's concept of frontiers of separation and contact. He believed that the functions of frontiers were to protect the state and allow the application of restrictions to safeguard defence, trade and health, and also to allow intercourse between the population of adjacent states. He therefore distinguished frontiers of separation from frontiers of intercourse or pressure and believed that generally 'natural barrier frontiers' developed within frontiers of separation while 'artificial boundaries' were drawn within frontiers of contact. This repeats Holdich's use of 'natural frontiers' and 'artificial boundaries' noted earlier. Nor does the generalization apply uniformly because frontiers of separation need not be related to features of the physical landscape but could be produced in flat country by the policies of neighbouring states. In classifying artificial boundaries Fawcett used the same three-fold system outlined by Curzon.

Fawcett concluded by identifying three trends observable at that time. First, he noted a growing precision of boundary definition and demarcation. Second, there appreared to be an increasing coincidence between political boundaries and linguistic limits: attempts were being planned to redraw Europe's boundaries to avoid minority problems. Lastly, Fawcett believed that there was a distinct tendency to place boundaries within frontiers of separation. Holdich had already shown that the second and third trends were contradictory in Europe, as the Versailles peace arrangements were to prove. In some cases the location of a boundary within a frontier of separation produced minorities as in the cases of Austria and Italy, and Czechoslovakia and Germany. In other cases the selected ethnographic boundary was unrelated to any physical features of the landscape.

There is no need to consider in detail Haushofer's boundary concepts outlined in 1927. He accepted Ratzel's view that boundaries were a measure of the state's power, and considered that it was the duty of the government to establish the strongest possible boundaries including an ethnically homogeneous population. The very wide definition of the area comprising German *Kultur* is well known, and it is interesting to recall that Haushofer proposed a military boundary (*Wehrgrenze*) beyond the cultural areas so that it could not be directly bombarded by enemy artillery. Like other students of boundaries, Haushofer attempted their classification, this time on a basis of state power which produced boundaries classified under the headings of attack, defence, growth and decay. Haushofer had little influence upon other workers in different countries and probably the main significance of the work in this respect is that it prompted a reply from Ancel in 1936 and 1938. These are considered after Lapradelle's work has been noted.

Lapradelle was a lawyer and his book published in 1928 dealt with borderlands and international law. This is one of the few studies considered here which does not apparently bear the imprint of the period in which it was written. On the other hand, the profession of its author is clearly represented in the precise language used, the careful documentation of examples and the simple plan employed.

Boundaries attract the interest of the international lawyer because they mark the position where states meet, and where international rights are determined and obligations assumed. While the boundary is a legal reality, Lapradelle agrees with Ratzel that the boundary cannot be considered out of the context of the borderland, and to allow this he distinguishes clearly between boundaries and frontiers. He makes the interesting observation that frontiers exist before and after boundary delimitation as zones having special political, legal and economic regulations. He agrees with Fawcett that the frontier is *un milieu de transformation* and goes on to suggest a triple division of frontiers based on Ratzel's original concept. Both authors believed that the zone of fusion or mingling in the frontier was bounded on both sides by the extreme peripheral zones of the neighbouring states. The central region is called *territoire limitrophe* by Lapradelle, and is the area where international law may apply; the peripheral flanking areas are called *frontières* and are subject to the internal laws of the states concerned. The total area of these three zones is called *le voisinage*. Accordingly Lapradelle deals firstly with the delimitation of boundaries and secondly with the legal organization of *le voisinage*.

Three stages in the evolution of a boundary are considered: preparation, decision and execution.

Les opérations de préparation précèdent la délimitation proprement dite. Le problème de la limite s'y trouve débattu sur le plan politique tout d'abord, sur le plan technique ensuite. Il s'agit, dans l'ensemble, de déterminer en dehors de tout débat territorial, le principe directeur suivant lequel le tracé sera décrit . . . La décision consiste dans la description de la limite, ou délimitation . . . L'exécution consiste à tracer sur le terrain la limite décrite et adoptée, opération qui porte le nom de démarcation.   (Lapradelle, 1928, p. 73)

This distinction of the stages of boundary evolution is one which geographers have now generally adopted (Jones, 1945). Boundaries were classified by Lapradelle into two groups based on their method of definition. Boundaries which were described by reference to some feature of the physical landscape were called *limites arti-ficielles dérivées*, mathematical boundaries were called *limites artificielles proprementdites*. The truly artificial boundaries were divided according to Curzon's system into astronomic, geometric and referential boundaries. It is strange that boundaries related to cultural features were not considered. It may be that the lawyer was concerned with the terms generally used in boundary treaties, but many boundaries drawn a few years earlier in Europe were based on ethnic features, even though the definitions might have made no reference to them. Certainly any comprehensive classification on this basis would have to take this third category into account, as Boggs (1940) showed.

The remainder of the book is concerned with reviewing the legal aspects of the organization of the three-fold border area, and showing how the interests of its citizens in respect of industry and pastoral farming are protected, and how the states collaborate in matters of trade, health and police regulations.

In the conclusion the zonal character of the border is emphasized, and a call is made for an objective study of the legal realities of borders, rather than the subjective study which believes that the entire state area is subject to the uniform application of internal laws.

Ancel (1938) wrote his book in answer to Haushofer's earlier study (1927), when the immediate troubled future of Europe could be plainly seen. The book was an amplification of a short study published in 1936. He criticized the German view that the boundary determined the position and territory of the state, which in turn determined its strength. Instead Ancel regarded the boundary as the result of state power generated by a particular political-social group rather than the cause. There seems to be little difference between these two views.

Ancel closely followed the views of Febvre in forming his concept of boundary studies.

Peu importe le marge c'est le coeur qu'il faut avant tout considérer.
(Febvre)

... ce n'est pas le cadre qui importe, mais ce qui est encadré.
(Ancel, 1938, p. 3)

For Ancel the boundary reflects the relationships between neighbouring groups and should be studied to this end rather than as a single element of the landscape. This continues the accepted idea that the boundary is a line within a borderland, and that the most meaningful geographical research results from their joint study. On the other hand, Ancel slightly overstates the case, for there is little chance that research into borderlands will be fruitful until a systematic study of the characteristics of boundaries has been made. This, however, may well be a point which was assumed by the classical French school of regional geographers.

The book is organized into three parts and in each case Ancel attempts to consider the boundaries of types of state rather than types of boundaries. In the first part amorphous states are considered under three headings – molecular societies, nomadic states and maritime empires. In dealing with the first two types it seems that Ancel is too concerned with describing the economy and way of life of the citizens rather than the limits of the socio-political groups. Even such groups as the Congolese often clearly distinguished the sovereign limits of the tribe, and many other tribes in Africa clearly marked their limits with fences and ditches and exercised partial control over peripheral zones beyond these defensive lines. Nor is it true to generalize that nomadic tribes do not have boundaries (Ancel, 1938, p. 28). It would be more true to say that sovereignty is vested in the nomads rather than the territory they own, but it is nevertheless a fact that nomadic tribes control the areas which their herds require and which their military strength can maintain. These limits will fluctuate, but at any particular time they would be clearly understood by neighbouring tribes. The treatment of maritime empires presents some interesting points about their organization and political geography but fails to demonstrate that the boundaries which limit their overseas possessions form a special class.

In the second and third parts Ancel considers *frontières plastiques* and *frontières mouvantes*. The concepts of Ratzel are attacked in introducing the consideration of moulded boundaries. Ratzel believed that the boundary was the peripheral organ of the state and that its fluctuations governed the strength or weakness of the state. Ancel maintains that the boundary results from pressures exerted from both sides and considers the line to be an equilibrium between two forces. It is difficult to see the difference between the two views. Surely if Ratzel's statement is applied to neighbouring states it follows that the boundary is the result of forces from each side. After examining the characteristics of medieval and modern boundaries, the latter being divided into physical and human types, Ancel proposes his concept of boundaries as lines of power equilibrium in greater detail. He suggests that boundaries may be likened to political isobars. This point again suggests that Ancel was much closer to the German position than he realized.

Gottman (1952, pp. 130–320) and Fischer (1957, p. 136) have attacked the biological metaphor on grounds of implication and accuracy. Isobars do not represent equalizations of two forces; they are lines of equal pressure drawn so that on one side air pressure is higher and on the other side lower. Ancel probably had in mind a line which was maintained in position by equal and opposite pressures from both sides. This is similar to Spykman's concept (1938) which regarded boundaries as the lines where state pressures were neutralized. Gottman also criticized the analogy because of the importance of physical factors at any given time in determining the position of isobars. The criticism was softened by reference to other books by Ancel where he showed complete awareness of the significance of human factors. Further, political boundaries do not have the fluidity of physical frontiers and it is dangerous to postulate that they do. Pressure against a boundary may result in a change of state functions rather than a change in boundary position.

In the final section Ancel examines the manner in which boundaries develop, the means by which they are maintained, and the factors which influence their advance or retreat, again relating his material to types of state rather than specific types of boundaries. Four definite conclusions followed from Ancel's work. He rejected the idea of natural boundaries based on physical features and historical precedent, and attacked the linear concept of boundaries. He then maintained that boundaries were lines of equilibrium owing their position at any time to the pressures exerted from either side, and again appealed for a consideration of boundaries as reflecting the relationship of neighbouring states.

> Il n'y a pas de problèmes de frontières. Il n'est que des problèmes de Nations. (Ancel, 1938, p. 196)

Ancel's book has apparently received little attention from subsequent workers and this may be due to the fact that he wrote as a Frenchman answering German territorial arguments which were threatening France as well as other European states. It is stated in the introduction that there is no intention of entering into debate with the geopoliticians, but the results may have been more effective and lasting if Ancel, with his known ability, had dissected their views as a geographer.

Boggs (1940) wrote his book at a time when the second world war was imminent and it may well be that the boundary problems associated with the origin of the war and its settlement prompted the book. Boggs began by examining the changing role of boundaries, showing how the self-imposed limits to which Lapradelle had referred had given way to boundary negotiations between adjacent states. The various functions applied to boundaries were listed, and it was noted that they were mainly negative rather than positive. He also measured the international boundaries within each continent and calculated the ratios between total boundary length and total area. He regarded this as a crude index of the interruptive quality of boundaries, allowing a comparison between continents. For example, Europe excluding the Soviet Union had an index of 7·3 miles of boundary for every 1,000 square miles, while the figure for North America was 1·3. Boggs continued this argument by accepting the concept that pressure against boundaries increases with numbers of persons living in the country. Therefore he multiplied the first index by the continental population density, and the figures for Europe and North America then became 1,400 and 27. While Boggs admitted that this was only a coarse measurement, he did a disservice to political geographers by suggesting that generalizations of this kind about boundaries had some value. This point was strongly criticized by Hinks (1940) who pointed out that the pressure against a boundary was often exerted against specific points rather than uniformly. Whittlesey may also have argued, from the premises which he advanced in 1944, that the total continental areas are not effectively subject to political authority. Fortunately few have tried to develop Boggs's idea of continental comparisons. The most recent attempt is by Hamdan (1963) who quotes Boggs's calculations in reviewing the political map of Africa, without making fresh calculations in the light of the many changes in the status of African boundaries. It is surprising that Hamdan decided to include the figures since they do not assist his argument, nor has he any excuse for making these continental generalizations since their defects have been made clear by Jones (1945).

The remainder of Boggs's book is much more satisfactory. After a chapter dealing with the classification and terminology of boundaries he examines the boundary problems associated with each continent. He also has a special chapter on water boundaries of which he had made an earlier detailed study (1937). There is one conceptual defect which should be mentioned. Boggs contended that

> one of the principal reasons for making any study of boundaries is the desire to determine what kinds of boundaries have proven to be 'good' and which have been found to be 'bad'.   (Boggs, 1940, p. 21)

This view again illustrates his tendency to generalize unrealistically about boundaries, for no boundaries are intrinsically good or bad.

Presumably he considers a boundary to be good if it is not the subject of dispute and bad if it occasions friction between the states on either side. But this view neglects the fact which had been clearly established by Ratzel, Lapradelle and Ancel, that the boundary is the meeting place of autonomous states and that their policies and actions determine the extent to which the border zone will be peaceful or troubled.

Il n'y a pas de 'bonne' ou de 'mauvaise' frontière: cela dépend des circonstances. La frontière des Pyrénées est aujourd'hui une frontière morte . . . Jadis, c'était une frontière de tension.   (Ancel, 1936, p. 210)

One would qualify Bowman's comment in the Foreword that the book by Boggs was a basic text. It was a very useful book which described the general features of the world's principal boundary problems at a time when the English-speaking world needed such a text, but the book did little to advance the study of boundaries by geographers. It fell short of the standards set by Lapradelle in his book and by Hartshorne in his papers on the boundaries of Upper Silesia and on boundary terminology. Boggs's book today is most frequently quoted for his exhaustive listing of state functions applied at the boundary, and the means by which boundaries may be defined.

In 1945 Jones published a very important book which dealt with the techniques of boundary-making. This book undoubtedly owed its inspiration to the knowledge that after the second world war many new boundaries would be drawn, but unlike many others which were products of their time, this book has a quality of being timeless in its approach. The comprehensive treatment of the subject will be continuously relevant to all who are connected with boundary construction. The work is carefully documented, and in the two main sections dealing with delimitation and demarcation there are many examples and a clear statement of the techniques for collecting material on which any decisions should be based. It is not only statesmen, treaty editors and boundary commissioners who profit from Jones's book, for the opening sections contain much of interest to the geographer. Perhaps the most important single point made by Jones is that boundaries are unique, that generalizations about them are not very valuable, and that it is not very profitable continually to search for means of classifying them.

> Each boundary is almost unique and therefore many generalizations are of doubtful validity.   (Jones, 1945, p. vi)

> It is possible therefore to classify boundaries and their functions in many ways. All share the artificiality of classification. The most real distinction between boundaries is between internal and international. The presence or absence of over-riding sovereignty is the basis.   (p.7)

> The process of boundary-making is smoothed by considering each boundary as a special case with individuality more pronounced than resemblance to a theoretical type.   (p. 11)

This is a most important point which had not been clearly made before, and which was timely, for many studies had aimed at general classifications of boundaries, and had derived from such classifications generalizations about state behaviour, and the significance and suitability of boundaries, which only applied to a fraction of the cases. It is regrettable that some geographers have persisted in their efforts to classify boundaries instead of making detailed studies of particular cases. While boundaries are unique they can be studied by the geographical techniques of field and library investigation which Jones noted.

The stages of boundary evolution examined by Jones were similar to those outlined by Lapradelle. These in turn relate to the allocation of political territory, the delimitation of a specific boundary site, and the demarcation of the boundary which may involve minor deviations. Jones added a fourth stage which involved the administration of the boundary and the maintenance of the boundary monuments and vistas.

The last author to be considered in this brief review is Fischer, whose contributions were published in 1949 and 1957. Both of Fischer's contributions are characterized by a lack of an apparent plan; too often it seems that random thoughts have been set down in their order of occurrence. A careful reading of these two studies suggests that Fischer is primarily concerned (i) with according proper recognition to the factors working for the continued stability of boundaries, and (ii) with an assessment of the way in which functions applied at the boundary may be so reduced that the boundary becomes obsolescent or so increased that the boundary begins to intrench itself into the landscape, thereby creating landscape differences which may be used as arguments for its retention. These are points worth making, but it is regretted that Fischer did not present them more clearly and with the support of detailed examples. Some of his generalizations do not bear close scrutiny.

> It has been pointed out that a boundary is unlikely to have remained in a fixed position if it did not coincide with some physical or human factor hospitable to it. But so far only physiographic features have drawn the attention of geographers working for persistence of boundaries. As a consequence 'artificial boundaries', i.e., those not naturally marked especially if they have lasted for a considerable time, have always been a difficult problem for geographers. They have tried to find formerly overlooked geographical foundations for selected artificial boundaries and have thereby gained valuable insights. In some cases, however, it remains doubtful whether the established geographical factor is not accidental and entirely insufficient to explain boundary location.
>
> (Fischer, 1949, p. 197)

The first sentence of this quotation presumably refers to international boundaries since discordant internal boundaries may persist for a considerable period. Even if this qualification is made, examination indicates that many discordant international boundaries, drawn by colonial powers in Africa and Arabia, have survived unaltered since they were drawn nearly a century ago. The second and third sentences do less than justice to the works of Jones (1932), Moodie (1943), Clifford (1936), Cornish (1936), and editors of treaty series such as Hertslet (1909) and Miller (1937), though admittedly not all of them were geographers. In view of the lack of any references in the last two sentences it is impossible to judge the validity of the statement, but the accepted geographic methods of tracing the evolution of the boundary through the original official treaty documents and correspondence should prevent such unsatisfactory results.

Later in the same work Fischer writes as follows:

> The tendency of internal boundaries to persist has been noticed more often than the same tendency of international boundaries.
>
> (Fischer, 1949, p. 202)

Sweeping statements of this order should be justified, but not only does Fischer fail to establish his case, he relies upon the example of federal boundaries of the United States, which surely form a special category of internal boundaries with many characteristics similar to international boundaries.

A more serious criticism of Fischer's work concerns his attempt to redefine the term 'frontier'. Fischer considers the 'frontier' to be that part of the state which extends inland from the boundary and merges imperceptibly with the state interior. He justifies this use of the term by the fact that frontiers between states, that is uncontrolled areas, have largely disappeared. Fischer refers to such historical features as 'boundary zones'. In the next chapter an attempt is made to clarify the use of the term 'frontier', and it must suffice here to deplore Fischer's suggestion, which complicates even his own writing. For example, what is the difference between 'transitional border zones', 'undelimited areas', 'boundary zone', 'undefined boundaries', and 'no-man's land boundary zone'?

This review suggests four conclusions. First, boundaries are of interest to workers in many fields. Lawyers, soldiers, and politicians have a practical interest in boundaries. For the lawyer they mark the area of contact between separate sovereignities and judicial systems. To the soldier they represent the first area which must be defended and the position from which attacks must be launched. Lastly, to the politician boundaries mark the limits of administration which should be maintained or extended, and the sensitivity of citizens to the state's boundaries make them a vital subject to politicians, since they can be used to generate national loyalty, as both Indonesian and German politicians have discovered. The interest of geographers, historians and political scientists is academic rather than practical although some of their work has been of value to lawyers and administrators. Geographers study boundaries because they are elements of the cultural landscape, and because they represent the limits of political sovereignty which is a meaningful areal quality varying over the Earth's surface. Furthermore, geographical factors often play a part in determining the position and form of boundaries, and the boundaries, once established, may exert some influence upon the landscape in which they lie. Historians study boundaries because they result from different policies in different periods and because they are often the cause of international disputes which have had far-reaching effect on historical trends. The political scientist is interested in boundaries as the legal definition of the state, and in the criteria by which they are established. Those political scientists who specialize in international affairs find boundaries a fruitful field of study in the contemporary scene as historians do for past periods.

Second, while most of the studies considered carry the imprint of the author's interest, which is expected, many also bear the clear marks of the period when the study was made. The preoccupation of Holdich with strong defensive boundaries surely is explained by the 1914–19 European war as well as by his imperial experience in India. In similar fashion Haushofer's work owed much to the depressed international position of Germany, and Ancel's answer was partly prompted by the increasing threat to French territory. This fact together with the divergent interests of the various authors has prevented the systematic advance of the subject and the construction of accepted concepts and a clearly understood terminology. For example, author after author, including Fischer in 1957, have attacked the concept of natural and artificial boundaries even though there was no confusion in Curzon's mind when he used the terms and even though the semantic defect had been made clear by Fawcett in 1918 and by Lapradelle in 1928. Another example is provided by Fischer's suggestion of a new meaning for the term 'frontier', at a time when there was some reason for hoping that the distinction between frontiers and boundaries was clearly understood by all workers, and the terms were being carefully used.

Third, one of the concepts which has been generally accepted is that the boundary must be considered in its territorial context. This view started with Ratzel, who saw the boundary as an abstraction and the boundary-zone as the reality, and has been continued. This is in accordance with geographic tradition for other linear features are considered in respect of surrounding areas. For example, the economic geographer is interested in the traffic generated in the area served by a railway, while the geomorphologist studies rivers in relation to the run-off provided by the catchment area and to the structure of the basin drained by the river. Ancel tried to go further than many by advocating the study of boundaries only to illustrate the relationship of the separated states. This is to emphasize a single aspect of boundary study and to neglect the boundary as an element of the landscape.

Fourth, one important concept which is slowly gaining acceptance concerns the originality of boundaries. Jones was the first writer to state clearly that attempts to generalize about boundaries are fraught with the danger of forming hypothetical concepts which do not correspond to any real case. Many earlier writers had spent much time in determining the best method of classifying boundaries. The trend has not apparently been eradicated, for Fischer has suggested a new method of classifying boundaries – by the extent to which they are recognized by states. This is surely a meaningless classification for geographers. The fact that the United States recognizes the boundaries of Estonia and Latvia as international boundaries is of no significance to the state functions applied at the boundary or the way in which the boundary influences the landscape.

From this selective review of the literature of boundary and frontier studies the following statement of geographical interest in the matter might be stated. Boundaries and frontiers are elements of the landscape which mark either the *de facto* or *de jure* limits of political sovereignty, which is one quality of areal differentiation. They are therefore objects of interest to both political geographers and regional geographers studying areas within which they occur. There are two aspects of boundary and frontier studies which are of interest to geographers, whether engaged in topical or regional studies. First, the position and character of any boundary or frontier is the resultant of the interaction of many factors, some of which are geographical, and best studied by geographers. Second, once any boundary or frontier is established it is capable of influencing the landscape of which it is a part and the development and policies of the separated states. This aspect is also a legitimate field of geographic inquiry.

There are two qualifications to this view. First, the geographer must be aware that workers from other fields will also be exploring the non-geographic factors involved in boundary and frontier evolution, and assessing the influence of the boundary and frontier on facets of human and state life which are not part of geography. For example, the geographer looks at the Sino-Indian dispute with a view to isolating those geographic factors of topography, colonization and settlement which have contributed to its development. The significance of the boundary dispute in respect of the construction of roads and defence works is also of interest, together with the extent to which economic projects in various parts of India are hindered by the transfer of funds to defence spending. On the other hand, historians are likely to trace the boundary policies of the British Raj, the various Chinese administrations and the present Indian Government, together with the significance of the contribution of the persons involved, such as Colonel Macmahon, the Dalai Llama, Mr Nehru and Mr Chou En-Lai. The political scientists for their part are interested in the interaction of two distinct forms of government, and the repercussions of the struggle on both administrations. Therefore the geographer must always be conscious that this is a shared field, and that geographical analysis alone will rarely provide the complete answer. The second point is a restatement of Jones's view on the uniqueness of boundaries and its extension to include frontiers. Geographers have spent too much time in devising classifications and generalizations about boundaries and frontiers which have led to little or no progress. It would seem more profitable for the geographer to make specific studies and to concentrate on the generation of a common body of techniques and concepts for treating such studies. In this of course the geographer must be continually aware of what is being done by other workers interested in the same field.

The remainder of this book is organized in the following way.

The second chapter considers frontiers and the remaining chapters deal with boundaries. The specific aspects of boundaries which are considered are their evolution, their influence on the landscape, disputes over boundaries, and internal boundaries. The separate treatment of internal boundaries is in response to Jones's view that the presence or absence of overriding sovereignty is the crucial basis of classifying boundaries. Each chapter is concluded by a case study designed to demonstrate the principles discussed earlier. Three of these examples are selected from Africa, where the author has carried out most of his fieldwork; one is from America; and the other from Australia.

An attempt has been made to use correctly such words as have a specific connotation in respect of boundaries and frontiers. A brief indication of these terms follows.

Boundary refers to a line, while *frontier* refers to a zone. The terms *allocation, delimitation* and *demarcation* are used in the sense outlined by Jones (1945). Allocation means the initial political division of territory. Delimitation means the selection of a boundary site and its *definition*. Demarcation refers to the construction of the boundary in the landscape. When a boundary has been demarcated it is *described* in the report of the Commission responsible. *Border-land* refers to the transition zone within which the boundary lies; it corresponds to Lapradelle's *voisinage*. It has not been found necessary to distinguish *le territoire limitrophe* from the flanking areas of *le voisinage*. Lastly there are the sequential terms proposed nearly thirty years ago by Hartshorne (1936). These terms describe the relationship between the boundary and the landscape through which it was drawn. An *antecedent* boundary was drawn before the development of most of the features of the cultural landscape, and if a boundary was drawn through an uninhabited area it was called a *pioneer* boundary. *Subsequent* boundaries were drawn after the development of the cultural landscape. If the boundary coincided with some physical or cultural divide it was described as *consequent* (Jones's suggestion for the extension of the term to cover cultural features is accepted). If, however, the boundary was not drawn within such a feature it was described as *superimposed*, for which the synonym *discordant* is occasionally used. A *relict* boundary is one which, although abandoned, is still marked by differences in the landscape which developed during its lifetime.

References

ANCEL, J., 1936, 'Les frontières: etude de géographie politique', *Recueil des Cours*, 55, pp. 207–97.

ANCEL, J., 1938, *Les frontières*, Paris.

BOGGS, S. W., 1937, 'Problems of water boundary definition: median lines and international boundaries through territorial waters', *Geogr. Rev.*, 27, pp. 445–56.

BOGGS, S. W., 1940. *International boundaries: a study of boundary functions and problems*, New York.

CLIFFORD, E. H. M., 1936, 'The British Somaliland-Ethiopian boundary', *Geogr. J.*, 51, pp. 289–307.

CORNISH, V., 1936, *Borderlands of language in Europe and their relation to the historic frontiers of Christendom*, London.

CURZON OF KEDDLESTON, LORD, 1907, *Frontiers*, The Romanes Lecture, Oxford.

FAWCETT, C. B., 1918, *Frontiers, a study in political geography*, Oxford.

FISCHER, E., 1949, 'On boundaries', *World Politics*, 1, pp. 196–222.

FISCHER, E., 1957, Chapters 4 and 5 in Weigert, H. W. and others, *Principles of political geography*, New York.

GOTTMAN, J., 1952, *La politique des états et leur géographie*, Paris.

HAMDAN, G., 1963, 'The political map of new Africa', *Geogr. Rev.*, 53, pp. 418–39.

HARTSHORNE, R., 1936, 'Suggestions on the terminology of political boundaries', *Annals*, Association of American Geographers, 26, pp. 56–7.

HAUSHOFER, K., 1927, *Grenzen*, Berlin.

HERTSLET, SIR E., 1909, *Map of Africa by Treaty*, H.M.S.O., London, 3 vols.

HINKS, A. R., 1940, Review, *Geogr. J.*, 96, pp. 286–9.

HOLDICH, COL. SIR T. H., 1916, *Political frontiers and boundary making*, London.

JONES, S. B., 1932, 'The forty-ninth parallel in the Great Plains: the historical geography of a boundary', *J. of Geography*, 31, pp. 357–67.

JONES, S. B., 1945, *Boundary-making, a handbook for statesmen*, Washington.

LAPRADELLE, P. DE, 1928, *La frontière: étude de droit international*, Paris.
LYDE, L. W., 1915, *Some frontiers of tomorrow: an aspiration for Europe*, London.
MILLER, H., 1931–7, *Treaties and other international acts of the United States of America*, 5 vols., Washington.
MOODIE, A. E., 1943, 'The Italo-Yugoslav boundary', *Geogr. J.*, 101, pp. 49–65.
RATZEL, F., 1895, *Politische Geographie*, Berlin.
SPYKMAN, N. J., 1938, 'Geography and Foreign policy', *American Political Science Review*, 32, pp. 28–50 and 213–36.

2

Frontiers

The term 'frontier' in political geography has two different meanings: it can refer to either the political division between two states or the division between the settled and uninhabited parts of one state. In either case the frontier may be considered as a line or a zone. While the context normally prevents confusion between the two meanings, problems of interpreting the sense can easily arise. It is for this reason that some geographers have attempted to restrict the use of the term to features possessing width, referring to simple linear divides as boundaries. Although the English, French (*la frontière* and *la limite*) and Italian (*il confine* and *la frontiera*) languages permit this convenient distinction, it has not been consistently employed by geographers.

Fawcett (1918) distinguished between the terms frontier and boundary, and did much to remove the confusion introduced by Holdich, who frequently referred to 'the boundaries which define the frontier', implying a carefully defined zone (Holdich, 1916). Behrens, in translating Adami's main work (Adami, 1927) used frontier for *confine* although footnotes in the book suggest that *confine* refers to a precise boundary, usually associated with the limits of private property, whereas *frontiera* refers to the limits of a state. In many cases Behrens uses frontier-line and boundary-line as synonyms. East (1937) called for the consistent use of frontier and boundary, but his exhortation was ignored by Boggs (1940), who admitted the distinction, but continued to use them as synonyms to avoid undue repetition. This practice was followed by the Royal Geographical Society (1951): a list of geographical definitions included two definitions of frontier, one of which was interchangeable with boundary. It was noted, however, that frontier-line was the correct alternative to boundary. Goblet (1955), as translated into English, used frontier to the complete exclusion of boundary, following the French tradition. East (with Wooldridge, 1951) made a further appeal for the careful use of the two terms, and his guidance in this respect is evident in a book published later (East and Moodie, 1956). More recently Weigert (1957) and Pearcy (1957) employ frontier to describe the area adjacent to the boundary, although Weigert notes that it may be used with reference to a border area preceding the delimitation and demarcation of a boundary. A recent theoretical study (Kristoff, 1959) does not consider the dimensional difference between boundaries and frontiers.

This brief review of a selection of boundary studies indicates that, although geographers have long recognized the distinction between a boundary and a frontier, this recognition has not been evident in writing. Further, the works of Weigert, Pearcy and Kristoff would suggest that the term frontier should refer to the transition zone, which stretches inwards from the boundary and merges impercep-tibly with the state core. They justify this change on the ground that precise boundaries have replaced vague frontiers throughout most of the world. Such a change would rob historical-political studies of clarity, and it is to be hoped that a term such as borderland will be used by these authors, leaving frontier to refer to zonal divisions between states.

The remainder of this chapter considers those aspects of frontiers which are of interest to geographers. The material is organized in two main parts. Settlement frontiers refer to frontiers *within* a state, separating settled and unsettled areas; political frontiers refer to frontiers *between* states.

Set lement frontiers

Settlement frontiers can exist only where *de jure* boundaries have been established to define the state area. The frontier then marks the limit to which the state's authority has extended in occupying its legally defined territory. Thus the American frontier, advancing through territory secured by treaty, falls into this category, while the Russian frontier, advancing eastwards through Asia, was a political frontier, marking the *de facto* limits of the Russian state, established by conquest. It seems worthwhile to distinguish the primary settlement frontiers of the classical American or Canadian examples from secondary settlement frontiers, which are found in nearly all countries today where attempts are being made to extend the habitable area. The two types have different characteristics.

Primary settlement frontiers are historical features, while secondary settlement frontiers are currently found in many countries where an adverse physical environment, or inadequate techniques, hinder further advance of land-use and settlement. The primary settlement frontier marked the *de facto* limit of the state's political authority, whereas the political authority of modern states extends beyond the secondary settlement frontiers, and can be exerted when necessary. Any state, such as Australia or the Republic of Sudan, which includes sections of desert provide examples of this situation. Special services are supplied for operation in the uninhabited areas if necessary. The range of potential economic activities in a primary frontier is generally greater than in the secondary frontiers. Fur trapping, timber felling, semi-subsistence cultivation, grazing, mining and manufacturing and service industries were all found at some point on the American frontier, or developed after it had passed. On the other hand, the advancement of secondary settlement frontiers is likely to be by the extension of irrigated farming, as in the Republic of Mali, by extensive ranching as in Rhodesia, or by the exploitation of mineral reserves as in parts of Canada.

Secondary frontiers normally reflect the limited range of economic activities by a population of low density, while on primary settlement frontiers, densities may be moderate to heavy. The American Census Bureau's definition of the frontier zone – areas having a population density of two to six persons per square mile – would have excluded many of the early frontiers in Georgia. The development of secondary frontiers is usually carefully planned, and based on a satisfactory communications network, in contrast to the haphazard development of primary frontiers, which were also characterized by 'rudimentary socio-political relations marked by rebelliousness, lawlessness and/or absence of laws' (Kristoff, 1959). Lastly the primary settlement frontiers were often advanced rapidly. In 1783, four million acres of the Cumberland Valley were sold in seven months, while in 1795, during only two months, 26,000 migrants crossed the Cumberland River in search of cheap land to the west (Billington, 1960). The advance of secondary settlement frontiers usually involves small areas and comparatively few people.

Much has been written about the primary settlement frontier, but there are only a few scattered references to secondary settlement frontiers. American historians are largely responsible for the thorough documentation of the American primary frontier, much of which is concerned with supporting or refuting Turner's frontier hypothesis, that the 'existence of an area of free land, its continuous recession and the advance of American settlement westward explain American development' (Turner, 1953). Indeed one suspects that historians have preempted the field, for geographic contributions are few. Whittlesey (East and Moodie, 1956), writing on the expansion and consolidation of the United States, makes only passing reference to the frontier and no reference to the detailed historical studies. Despite this situation, geographers can make a real contribution beyond the mapping of frontier phenomena, which has been done for the American and Canadian frontiers (Paullin, 1932 and Adams, 1943, Kerr, 1961).

The position of the frontier, which represents the *de facto* zonal limit of political authority, and its width, are of prime interest to geographers. In order to determine the frontier's extent some criteria must be developed to distinguish it from non-frontier areas. A simple basis of population density is unsatisfactory, and a more satisfactory measure is likely to be found in the degree of economic and political organization. This is a task calling for training in historical and political geography. Information about the position of the frontier at any time will give some indication of the factors which have influenced the frontier's rate of advance.

Any advance of the frontier probably resulted from a combination of factors, which can be principally divided into forces of attraction based on the nature of the environment, and forces of pressure from the frontier hinterland. The role of unusually favourable soil groups, such as are found in the Blue Grass country of Kentucky and the cotton lands of the Gulf plains, in promoting the rapid advance of the American frontier, are well known. In a similar fashion, discoveries of precious mineral deposits have caused spectacular frontier advancement, as for example in the Transvaal. Pressures within the frontier hinterland take many forms. Turner (1953) and Billington (1960) have shown how many of the frontiersmen were seeking to avoid high land-prices, heavy taxation, and political and religious disabilities, imposed either by the first, well-established settlers or by the governments of the country of origin. Further, the experience gained on one frontier in respect of land legislation, mining laws and Indian treaties, was applied at subsequent frontiers and often allowed speedier settlement of these problems. Periods of standstill or retreat along the frontier resulted either from the unfavourable nature of the environment or the inadequacy of techniques for utilizing it, the armed resistance of indigenous groups, or the preoccupation of the state with more urgent considerations.

In these successive frontiers we find natural boundary lines which have served to mark and affect the characteristics of the frontiers, namely: the 'fall-line'; the Alleghany Mountains; the Mississippi; the Missouri where its direction approximates north-south; the line of the arid plains, approximately the ninety-ninth meridian; and the Rocky Mountains. The fall line marked the frontier of the seventeenth century; the Alleghanies that of the eighteenth; the Mississippi that of the first quarter of the nineteenth; the Missouri that of the middle of this century (omitting the Californian movement); and the belt of the Rocky Mountains and arid tract, the present frontier. Each was won by a series of Indian wars.   (Turner, 1953, p. 9)

The maps of Indian battles (Paullin, 1932) show that the fiercest resistance by indigenes often coincides with the most difficult terrain, which offers excellent strategic opportunities for defence. It was in the scrub country of Queensland that aborigines offered the greatest resistance to the extension of pastoral activities. In Kamerun during the early years of this century the Germans faced their greatest problems in pacifying the Chamba and other pagan groups, located in the heavily dissected borderland with Nigeria. The stagnation of the American frontier during the twenty years before 1795 resulted from the preoccupation of the Colonies with securing independence, establishing a federal constitution and defeating the Indians in the area already settled.

In some cases attempts were made to halt frontier advance, by the government or by interested trading organizations. Some of the earliest coastal states in North America sought to restrict the frontier advance, in order to retain political power, and to avoid a further drain of their population. In the hinterland of New York and Pennsylvania, the Iroquois Confederation blocked for a century the route through the Catskill and Berkshire Ranges, by the Mohawk and Hudson Valleys, in order that the Indians who supplied their fur trade should not be driven away (Billington, 1960).

Turner maintains that 'each frontier leaves its traces behind it, and when it becomes a settled area the region still partakes of the frontier characteristics' (Turner, 1950, p. 4). This suggests a fruitful field for geographical research. Can any elements of the cultural landscape be attributed to the period when the area was a primary settlement frontier? There is probably a connexion between present property boundaries and the original policies of land allocation and appropriation. It seems unlikely that the present economy will reveal many features which can be traced to frontier times, since the earliest economic activities of hunting and grazing will survive only if the land is unsuitable for cultivation, and lacks resources on which can be built a range of towns, with well-developed secondary and service industries. It has been noted by Clarke (1959) that when a period of frontier standstill allowed an accumulation of population as in Georgia and Tennessee, eventual advance was more orderly and complete. Rapid advance, without resistance, resulted in scattered and discontinuous settlement patterns. It would be interesting to know whether settlement analysis reflects this process of development.

Secondary settlement frontiers are found in all countries which include areas of unfavourable environment, such as tropical or temperate desert, heavily dissected uplands, or thick tropical rain forest: and areas which require the use of advanced and often expensive techniques, if they are to be used for purposes other than mineral extraction. These are the areas which are bypassed by the primary frontier, concerned with rapid advance, exploitation and profit. They will be attacked later if circumstances require it, and new techniques or discoveries make it possible to revalue the environment. Burt has recorded that in the mid-nineteenth century 'the expansion of Canadian settlement ran up against the rocky Pre-Cambrian Shield, with the result that the Canadian frontier movement crossed the (American) border, where it became merged in the greater movement to the northern Middle Western States' (Wyman and Kroeber, 1957). Only when the availability of land in the American West was reduced did the frontier cross the boundary again, allowing the development of western Canada. In many European states only short secondary frontiers surround small sectors of unfavourable environment. In Australia on the other hand, the long secondary settlement frontier developed on the site of the last primary frontier, around the central desert. Attempts to thrust forward secondary frontiers usually depend on some incentive, such as shortage of land, shortage of food in time of war, strategic needs, or the discovery of new mineral deposits. Shortage of land in African Reserves in southern Matabeleland has led to the cultivation of land where there is a high risk of drought or rainfall deficiency. In Java, population pressure on available land resources has caused the cultivation of slopes with a high erosion hazard. In many cases efforts to advance secondary settlement frontiers are guided and controlled by government, because of the need for considerable capital expenditure without rapid yields.

Examples of the part played by improved and new techniques, are found in South Africa and Australia. The waterless areas of the Kalahari sandveld were not settled until after 1903, when the well-drill made it possible to tap underground water reserves, which could be brought to the surface by wind-pumps. The Australian example concerns Kangaroo Island, ninety miles south-west of Adelaide (Bauer, 1953). This island attracted few early settlers because of the failure of grain and clover crops and the susceptibility of sheep and cattle grazed there to 'coast disease'. Just before the second world war tests revealed that the application of super-phosphate and copper sulphate ensured satisfactory crop yields and eliminated coast disease. Settlement of returned servicemen has been fostered by the Land Development Executive, of the Department of Lands of South Australia, a State which is not conspicuously endowed with areas of reliable rainfall. The Executive clears, ploughs and seeds the land before occupation, and continues to offer advisory services afterwards. In the decade following the second world war 222,000 acres were cleared on the island. The spectacular extension of cultivation in Soviet Asia was stimulated during World War II by the need to produce food to replace supplies denied by German occupation. Subsequent economic developments offer the strategic advantage of creating centres of production remote from potential land-based attacks (East and Spate, 1961, and Hooson, 1962).

Nearly a century ago the threat of Russian advance into Hokkaido encouraged the Japanese Government to foster the rapid colonization of that island. The government distinguished between those immigrants who travelled independently, and those who travelled with the aid of a government subsidy. Independent farmers received implements, seed and ten yen for every quarter-acre cleared. Subsidized farmers received a rice ration for three years in addition to seed and implements. Their bonus for clearing land was two yen per quarter-acre. Independent artisans and merchants received a gift of 150 yen and a free yearly bonus of fifty yen for three years. Subsidized artisans received an initial grant of 120 yen, and an annual bonus of fifty yen for three years, which eventually had to be repaid (Harrison, 1953). In the decade following 1869 nearly 65,000 Japanese immigrants entered Hokkaido.

The discovery of new mineral deposits, or the change in world trading conditions which makes the mining of known deposits possible, have often caused the advance of a secondary settlement frontier, especially in arctic zones or tropical deserts. In north-west Mauretania there is a scheme for the open-cast mining of iron ore in the Kedia d'Idjil Range, from deposits which total 110 million tons of high-grade ore. The construction of a town near Tazadit has begun, and its population in 1965 is expected to be 6,250. The town is to be supplied with water drawn from a depth of 130 feet and will be connected to Port Etienne, 400 miles away, by rail and road (Church, 1961).

Political frontiers

The essential difference between settlement and political frontiers is that there is no *de jure* boundary beyond the political frontier. Settlement frontiers disappear when they reach the furthermost *de jure* limits; political frontiers will only disappear when two or more states compete for territory and delimit a boundary separating their areas of sovereignty. Geographic interest in political frontiers is mainly concerned with their physical characteristics, their position, the attitudes and policies of the states separated by the frontier, the influence of the frontier on the subsequent development of the cultural landscape, and the way in which boundaries are drawn within the pre-existing frontiers.

Lord Curzon (1907) and Holdich (1916) classified frontiers into two groups – natural and artificial. The following quotations indicate their confusion of language.

> From Natural Frontiers I pass to the category of Artificial Frontiers, by which are meant *those boundary lines*, which, not being dependent upon natural features of the earth's surface for their selection, have been artificially or arbitrarily created by man.
>
> (Curzon, 1907, p. 23, emphasis added)

> Frontiers and *the boundaries which define the frontiers* may be classed under two heads, natural and artificial.
>
> (Holdich, 1916, p. 147, emphasis added)

East (1937) has convincingly shown the unsatisfactory nature of this dual division. All political frontiers and boundaries require selection and are therefore artificial or arbitrary. The suggestion has been made that frontiers could be classified into 'living' and 'dead' categories. A dead frontier is one separating states which have reached equilibrium and no longer exert pressure against the frontier. A living frontier is one still subject to pressure from one or both sides. Such a classification would be difficult to apply, since it would be necessary to establish some minimum measurement of pressure to group the frontiers under consideration satisfactorily. A more serious defect is the connotation carried by the term 'dead': that the frontier serves no function, whereas it is clearly possible for a frontier to be stable and yet for states to exercise rigorously their functions near the frontier, and for a considerable volume of trade to cross it.

Lord Curzon's essay contained the seeds of a classification which were brought to fruition by East. He distinguished between frontiers of contact and frontiers of separation, and observed that 'states have always sought frontiers which foster separation from, rather than assimilation with, their neighbours' (East, 1937). Some frontiers, either by the attraction of their resources, or the ease with which they can be crossed, allow contact between separated political groups. This contact may take the form of trade, migration or conflict. On the other hand, the frontier may possess physical characteristics which make it unattractive to exploiters, and difficult for travellers. In no case, however, does the geography of the frontier determine the degree of intercourse between states; rather the attitudes and policies of the divided states are determinative. When Chile achieved independence its state limits included the Atacama Desert to the north and the Andes Mountains to the east, both physical barriers which inhibited cultural contacts. Yet, during the last century the expansionist policies of the Chilean Government carried the country into war with Peru and Bolivia, over the Tacna-Arica districts of the Atacama, and into a dispute with Argentina concerning the trans-piedmont slopes of the Andes, which were in some cases settled by Chilean emigrants. The successful northward advance against Peru and Bolivia, made for economic and strategic reasons, delivered to Chile the port of Arica and access to valuable borax, copper and nitrate deposits (Dennis, 1931).

The effects of a policy of isolation are revealed by considering the case of the Benin kingdom west of the Niger Delta. Although the forested frontiers surrounding Benin were no more difficult to traverse than similar frontiers surrounding other indigenous kingdoms, there was no contact between European traders and Benin because traders were not welcomed. Eventually it required an expeditionary force to conquer the country, and to establish relations between the colonial and indigenous authorities in 1897.

Political frontiers between states have generally been replaced by boundaries throughout the world. Only in the eastern Arabian desert is there an absence of boundaries delimiting the territories of the states. Political frontiers existed before boundaries, and the best current examples are to be found between tribal territories *within* some African and South American states. Research into political frontiers must therefore have a strong historical and anthropological basis. Political frontiers generally enjoyed less intensive economic development than the territories they separated. This was because the environment was less favourable, or because the resources of the existing state area were sufficient, or because it was the policy of the state to neglect the frontier, thereby enhancing its divisive character. Deserts, mountain ranges, rivers and river plains, and woodlands have all formed frontiers at some stage in history. It follows from this that the frontiers were usually less densely populated than the flanking states, and that the inhabitants of the frontier, if any, enjoyed a lower standard of living. Tacitus (*Germania*, 46) describes the debased condition of the Slavic Venedi, who occupied the woody and mountainous area between the Peucini and Fenni, while a more recent example was cited by Tilho (*Ministère des Colonies*, 1910), namely the wretched Bedde pagans, who occupied the swampy areas between the Bornu and Sokoto kingdoms in the western Sudan.

Where there was the threat of invasion or trespass, political frontiers were selected for their defensive advantages and this point was thoroughly discussed by Curzon and Holdich. Curzon mentioned that deserts formed the best defensive frontiers, but it seems worth remarking that the extensive deserts such as the Sahara were often the habitat of mobile and warlike tribes such as the Tuareg, which plagued the surrounding semi-agricultural tribes.

> So long as hungry tribesmen inhabit barren and almost waterless hills, which command open and fertile plains, so long will they resort to plundering incursions in order to obtain the necessaries of life.
>
> (Davies, 1932, p. 179)

Linear mountain ranges and rivers had the strategic advantage of allowing the defending forces to focus their strength at passes and bridges. The possession of limiting deserts, mountain ranges and major rivers is a matter of fortune, and it seems likely that many of the original frontiers consisted of woodland and marshes. The swamps and forests surrounding Westphalia played a major part in the defeat of some Roman legions (Tacitus, *Annales*, i, pp. 61 and 63). A more modern illustration was provided by the forested margins of Kikuyuland in East Africa. This forested zone was about two hours march in width, and enabled the Kikuyu to destroy the Masai invaders, who seemed invincible on the grassy plains of Masailand (Höhnel, 1894, 1).

Many states tried to mark their frontiers by one or another means. The famous Roman and Chinese walls are the best examples. The Great Wall of China served not only to exclude nomadic barbarians but also to restrict the number of Chinese who adopted a modified agricultural system, and became more difficult to control from the Chinese capital (Lattimore, 1940). The walls of the Roman Empire, unlike the Great Wall of China, did not mark a major environmental divide and seemed to be built solely for the defence of the Empire by permitting some control, if not exclusion, of the barbarians. Where clear physical features were not available, the Romans constructed walls such as the well-known Hadrian's wall, linking Solway Firth and the Tyne. Two others were built across the re-entrant formed by the upper courses of the Rhine and Danube, and east of the Drava-Danube confluence. The barbarians north of the Roman wall also built earthworks to delimit their territory. It is recorded that the Angrivarii constructed a broad earthwork to mark their boundary with the Cherusci. It might be asked whether these walls were not boundaries rather than frontiers, even though they were unilaterally selected. The reply would be that generally the walls formed not the limit of sovereignty, but rather the first or last line of defence in depth (Baradez, 1949). The Roman walls were reinforced by establishing farmers on land behind the wall, in a zone called *agri limitanei*. These men were expected to assist the defence of the wall in time of need. An exception to this general rule was noted by Collingwood (1923), who maintains that the *vallum* behind Hadrian's wall marked the limit of Rome's civil government.

The counterparts of the Roman and Chinese walls could be found in Africa until quite recently:

The kingdom was surrounded, where there were no natural defences, by deep and wide ditches defended by tree trunk pallisades and crossed at intervals by narrow bridges. The northern frontier was formed by the Gojeb river, called Godafo by the Kafa. Bieber gives the dimensions of the ditches as 6 metres in width and 3 metres in depth; he describes the gates, *kello*, as consisting of circular fenced enclosures entered by drop gates. Customs dues were collected at these gates. Outside the line of fences was a strip of unoccupied land like the *moga* of the Galla states. At points where Galla attacks were expected, the gates were additionally defended by a high rampart and several lines of entrenchment, a form of defence much admired by the neighbours of the Kafa.

(Huntingford, 1955, p. 116)

The *moga*, or uncultivated strip, of the Galla states of the Horn of Africa was inhabited only by fierce brigands, who were encouraged by the Galla rulers to attack common enemies and recapture escaped slaves.

Fischer maintains that a 'rather extensive literature deals with the development of boundary lines out of such (frontier) zones or related features' (Weigert, 1957). However the works which he cites do not treat this aspect of boundaries in detail. The general impression is that as states separated by frontiers extend their territory, the unclaimed land diminishes. Eventually property disputes arise, and an attempt is made to resolve these difficulties by delimiting a precise boundary. No doubt this situation has occurred in many cases, but there are some significant variations on this theme, which are examined in the following paragraphs.

We can begin by saying that frontiers normally diminish in width and that frontiers of separation are replaced by frontiers of contact. Frontiers can diminish through one of two processes: incorporation of parts of the frontier by one or both flanking states, or the creation of subsidiary political organizations within the frontier.

Annexation of parts of the frontier might take place because of land hunger in the state, or through the development of new techniques which enable the frontier resources to be revalued. Amongst the Somali, who occupy the Horn of Africa, the frontiers between tribal grazing areas are in a constant state of flux, since occupance and military competence are the sole criteria of ownership. As the herds grow or decline in size so the amount of pasture required increases or diminishes, producing variation in frontier width. If the frontier existed because of the internal weakness of the flanking states, or the preoccupation of these states with threats from other quarters, the removal of the threat or the resolution of internal weaknesses may allow the frontier to be appropriated. Alternatively, the frontier may be invaded and incorporated for strategic reasons. For example, after the Roman successes in Gaul, the eastern flank of this advance was protected by the annexation of Noricum, Pannonia, Moesia and Dacia in the Danube Basin. This advance also removed the scene of conflict from the Mediterranean centres of the Empire (East, 1950). In some cases annexation for one reason carried additional benefits. The Romans invaded the area between the River Rhine, the River Main and the Taunus ridge in order to stop the raids of the Chatti. They then discovered that the area possessed hot springs and iron and silver deposits.

The subsidiary organizations which can be created within the frontier include marches, buffer states, and spheres of interest or influence. A march is a border territory organized on a semi-permanent military system to defend the frontier. An illustration of the creation of marches, or marks, can be seen in the policies of Charlemagne and Otto.

> From these Marks, intended to safeguard the Frontiers of the Empire from Slavonic or alien contact, and ruled by Markgrafs or Markgraves, sprang nearly all the kingdoms and states which afterwards obtained an independent national existence, until they became either the seats of empires themselves, as in the case of the Mark of Brandenburg, or autonomous members of the German Federation.
>
> (Curzon, 1907, p. 27)

The Carolingian Empire was protected from the Slavs and Avars by a series of marches stretching from the Baltic Sea to the Adriatic Sea – Sorbia, Bohemia, Moravia, Pannonia (formerly a Roman frontier Province), and Friuli. In the west and south respectively the marches of Brittany and Spain guarded the Empire at the neck of the Breton peninsula and the eastern Pyrenees.

Buffer states have been constructed in frontiers when it was desired to reduce the possibility of conflict between two powerful states. The territorial integrity of the buffer state was normally guaranteed by either the flanking powers or some third power. Marshall-Cornwall (1935) discusses several cases of buffer-states in Asia, but some of his examples, such as Sikkim and Bhutan, seem to resemble Protectorates where former British and present Indian Governments have undertaken to protect the territories, in return for some measure of influence in their foreign relations. In any event most of the cases discussed seem to refer to the guarantee of states already in existence. Uruguay seems to be a genuine case of a buffer state being created within a potentially dangerous frontier of contact. Portuguese and Spanish interests conflicted north of the River Plata, and, after negotiations in which Britain was involved, both contestants agreed to the creation of Uruguay as a neutral state. Another example was provided through the creation, by Britain and France, of a neutral state, between the Mekong and Salween Rivers, to separate British interests in Burma from French interests in Indo-China. The neutral zone serves the same function as the buffer state, but the area is not constituted into a separate political unit. It is either administered by one or both flanking states. Neutral zones exist today between Saudi Arabia and Kuwait and Saudi Arabia and Iraq. In 1887 Britain and Germany separated their spheres of influence in Togoland and the Gold Coast by a neutral zone stretching north of the confluence of the Dakka and Volta Rivers.

The concepts of spheres of interest and influence developed during the last century, when the major European powers were establishing actual and potential claims to parts of Asia and Africa. At no time have the responsibilities assumed under either concept by the claimant powers been defined. Both concepts are means of reserving a portion of territory from the political interference of another state, and it has been assumed that a sphere of interest is a less significant claim than a sphere of influence. Holdich (1916, p. 96) suggests that a sphere of interest becomes a sphere of influence when there is the threat of competition by another state, but against this it must be said that the formal definition of both spheres of interest and of influence were found usually in bilateral territorial agreements. An example is provided by the second article of the Anglo-French Agreement of 1890, in respect of African territories:

The Government of Her Britannic Majesty recognizes the sphere of influence of France, to the south of her Mediterranean possessions up to a line drawn from Say on the Niger to Barruwa on lake Tchad, drawn in such a way as to comprise in the sphere of action of the Niger Company all that properly belongs to the kingdom of Sokoto.

(Hertslet, 1909, p. 730)

At the time of this Agreement Monteil was the only Frenchman to have visited the area, whereas the Royal Niger Company had agents at the court of the Emir of Sokoto. The degree of interference with the indigenous organizations in the sphere of interest or influence varied in almost every case. At one end of the scale, the European Power assumed no responsibilities, but claimed the exclusive right of its nationals to trade in the area: at the other end there was a high degree of political control more appropriate to the condition of a Protectorate.

It was noted earlier that one aspect of geographical research connected with settlement frontiers concerned identifying elements in the landscape derived from frontier origins. Such studies are also a proper facet of political frontier studies, although little has been done in this direction by geographers. The best studies are by Cornish (1936) and Wilkinson (1955). Cornish traced the evolution of the language borderlands of Europe, such as Flanders, Lorraine, Friuli, Istria and Macedonia. He found that in each case the language frontier coincided with an earlier political frontier between Christendom and heathen states, which had been static for some time. The growth of polyglot language regions occurred only where the frontier did not coincide with a divisive physical feature. Cornish called such regions link-lands, to characterize their position between larger state areas. The heathen languages were eventually reduced to writing through contact with Christianity, and their traditions were thus preserved. Cornish points out that only during the nineteenth century, with improved means of mass communication between the larger state areas and the link-lands, did the bonds of language become more important than the regional ties of the link-lands.

Wilkinson shows how the Jugoslav Kosmet, at various times, formed the frontier between the Eastern and Western parts of the Roman Empire, the Bulgar and Byzantine Empires, Christianity and

Islam, and Yugoslavia and Albania. This situation has resulted in some neglect of the economic resources of the area and hindered its integrated development. Problems have arisen when boundaries have been drawn through upland areas which provide the summer pastures of a transhumance economy.

In view of the paucity of detailed geographical studies concerned with political frontiers it seems worthwhile to record the author's research in West Africa. The following account is based on fieldwork and a review of a very extensive literature, of which the most important works were by Barth (1857), Staudinger (1889), and Hogben (1929).

Frontiers in the Niger-Benue area

The largest state in West Africa was the Sokoto-Gando Empire, founded by the Fulani Jihad at the beginning of the nineteenth century (Fig. 1). This Empire stretched from Libtako in the west to Adamawa in the east, and from Katsina in the north to the latitude of Ilorin in the south. This territory, which was not subject to uniform political authority, was organized into Provinces, each having a degree of independence, which varied directly with their distance from Sokoto or Gando. In the provinces of Zaria, Bida, Kontagora, Nassarawa, Kano and Muri, the Fulani subjugated the indigenous tribes. In other areas such as Bauchi and Western Adamawa, enclaves of pagan groups retained their independence on hilltop settlements. Finally, in Libtako and eastern Adamawa, only the main towns on the principal trade routes were subject to Fulani authority. These Fulani towns were exclaves within uncontrolled pagan areas, and might have been described as marchtowns.

North and west of Sokoto lay the *Habe* states, organized by Hausa chiefs who continued the struggle against the Fulani from new capitals. The westernmost *Habe* state was Kebbi, which had a narrow frontier with Sokoto and Gando, in the neighbourhood of which many raids were carried out and battles fought. The other two *Habe* states, Gober and Maradi, were separated from Sokoto by a frontier of separation, formed from a devastated zone. The towns of Jankuki, Dankama and Madawa were destroyed by Fulani attacks. This depopulated zone became more thickly wooded than the rest of the area, and served as a refuge for robbers. On the northern fringes of this frontier, Maradi established the marches of Gazawa and Tessawa.

North-east and east of Sokoto lay the Bornu Empire and its vassal states, which included Zinder. The reduced power of Bornu after the Fulani conquest and subsequent Bornu revival had increased the degree of autonomy enjoyed by its traditional northern tributary states, including Zinder. Between Kano Province of the Sokoto-Gando Empire and Zinder, there was a deserted frontier of separation, resulting from the weakness of both states. There were only occasional raids across this frontier by both flanking states. The frontier of separation dividing Bornu from Sokoto can be divided into three parts. North of the River Gana lived the Bedde pagans, protected by a forested, swampy environment. Armies from both Sokoto and Bornu conducted slave raids against these people. Between the River Gana and the Mandara Mountains the forested frontier of separation was defended on the Bornu side by a series of quasi-independent marches, which had a long history of resistance to the Fulani. The Mandara Mountains themselves formed the third section of the frontier of separation, between Bornu and Adamawa. This area was occupied by the Marghi pagans, against whom the Fulani exerted intermittent pressure. The continued independence of the Marghi was advantageous to Bornu, since it prevented possible collision with the Adamawa Fulani, and discouraged slaves from escaping southwards.

The southern frontier of the Sokoto-Gando Empire marked the broad division between the states of the Sudan and those of the forested zone. In the west Gando had a common frontier with the kingdom of Borgu. Westwards from Yelwa, on the south side of the River Niger, there was a narrow frontier of contact against which the Fulani exerted continuous pressure unsuccessfully. Between Yelwa and Jebba the River Niger flows through a series of deep gorges, which effectively separated the two states. This frontier was continued westwards from Jebba into a hilly, forested zone.

There was an unstable frontier of contact between Ilorin Province of the Gando Empire and the Yoruba states of the south. Both states maintained permanent armies against each other, and the

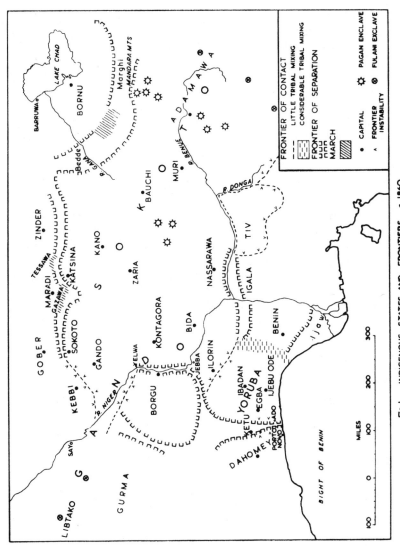

Fig. 1 INDIGENOUS STATES AND FRONTIERS c. 1860

FRONTIER OF CONTACT
LITTLE TRIBAL MIXING
CONSIDERABLE TRIBAL MIXING
FRONTIER OF SEPARATION
MARCH

● CAPITAL
∧ FRONTIER INSTABILITY
✿ PAGAN ENCLAVE
⊗ FULANI EXCLAVE

BARRUWA
LAKE CHAD
BORNU
Morghi
MANDARA MTS

Bedde
ZINDER
TESSAWA
MARADI
GAZAWA
GOBER
KATSINA
KANO
ZARIA
BAUCHI
MURI
R. BENUE
R. GONGOLA
ADAMAWA

SOKOTO
GANDO
KEBBI
SAY
LIBTAKO
GURMA
G
A
R. NIGER
BORGU
KONTAGORA
BIDA
KELWA
JEBBA
ILORIN
NASSARAWA
IGALA
R. DONGA
TIV

YORUBA
IBADAN
KETU
EGBA
IJEBU ODE
DAHOMEY
PORTO NOVO
LAGOS
BENIN
Ijaw

BIGHT OF BENIN

MILES
100   0   100   200   300

position of the frontier depended upon their relative strength at any time. Eastwards this frontier broadened into one of separation between the Fulani of Kabba and the Benin kingdom, resulting partly from weakness of the Fulani and partly from the isolation policy of Benin. At intervals both states raided the frontier for slaves, further fragmenting the small Yoruba groups living there. This frontier of separation was continued east of the River Niger between Nassarawa Province of the Gando Empire and the Igala tribes. The frontier zone lay generally south of the Benue and was flooded with refugees from the north bank, which was effectively conquered by the Fulani. The tribes of the south were protected by the river except at periods of low flow, when the Fulani raiders could easily cross. The Benue formed the frontier of separation between the Tiv and Fulani states, except for a small holding which the Tiv maintained on the north bank of the river. The stability of this frontier resulted partly from the sturdy independence of the Tiv, and partly from their traditional friendship with the Fulani. The other frontiers of the Tiv group were remarkably unstable frontiers of contact, resulting from the outward migration of the Tiv, which involved the absorption of the farmlands of the Igala and Ogoja tribes.

It now remains to describe the common frontier of the four recognizable forest-states. The weakness of Borgu, together with the conflicts of the Yoruba Confederation with the Ilorin Fulani, and Dahomey, resulted in Borgu being limited to the south by a wide forested frontier of separation, which was unpopulated except for some brigands. Between Egba, the westernmost Yoruba state, and Dahomey a frontier of separation narrowed towards the coast – the target for both states, seeking to dominate trade between the Europeans and the interior. Both armies made frequent raids into the frontier during the dry season when rivers posed no obstacles. The Ewe-speaking refugees from the west and the Egbado refugees from the east formed a complex ethnic mixture in the frontier. The distinction between Yoruba and Benin territory was not a sharp one. The peaceful frontier contained a complex intermixture of both groups, gradually shading to Yoruba dominance to the west and Benin dominance to the east.

It is impossible, at the present time, to determine the extent of the Benin Empire at any particular period of the past. The frontiers were continually expanding and contracting as new conquests were made and as vassals in the border rebelled and were reconquered.

(Bradbury, 1957, p. 21)

To the south of Benin the delta tribes, such as the Ijaw, preserved their independence largely as a result of the defensive character of the swamps and creeks. By the middle of the last century the policy of isolation had caused Benin to withdraw its authority from the western bank of the Niger. East of the Niger the political organization of the Ibo did not rise above the level of the clan or family. While some of these groups must have been surrounded by areas of unclaimed forest, their distribution cannot be reconstructed at the present scale of inquiry.

There seem to be three main results of the former location of past frontiers in the present landscape. First, the colonial boundaries which were superimposed on the indigenous political fabric did coincide to some extent with the indigenous frontiers. The Anglo-French boundary between Dahomey and Lagos was drawn within the frontier between Dahomey and Egba. The Anglo-French boundary between Niger and Northern Nigeria showed some correspondence with the devastated sections of the frontier between Sokoto and the northern *Habe* states of Maradi and Zinder. The present federal boundary between Western and Northern Nigeria is clearly related to the northern boundary of the former Yoruba and Benin kingdoms. Second, pressure from both flanks of some frontiers of separation has created ethnic shatter zones. The ethnic complexities of the areas between the former Dahomey and Egba kingdoms, between the Kabba and Benin kingdoms, and between Nassarawa and the Igala tribes are revealed in the striking variations over short distances, in house types and agricultural methods. Third, these shatter zones, marginal to the cores of the original states and their colonial successors, and lacking unified political control, have remained underdeveloped, and have not shared in the extension of services which have characterized other areas.

References

ADAMI, V., 1927, *National frontiers in relation to international law*. Trans. T. T. Behrens, London.

ADAMS, J. T., 1943, *Atlas of American History*, New York.

BARADEZ, J., 1949, *Fossatum Africae*, Paris, Arts et metiers graphiques.

BARTH, H., 1857, *Travels and discoveries in north and central Africa*. London.

BAUER, F. H., 1953, 'Government land development on Kangaroo Island,' *Proceedings of the Royal Geographical Society of Australasia*, 53, pp. 1–18.

BILLINGTON, R. A., 1960, *Westward expansion*, 2nd ed., New York.

BOGGS, S. W., 1940, *International boundaries*, New York.

BRADBURY, R. E., 1957, *The Benin Kingdom*, International African Institute, London.

CHURCH, R. J. H., 1961, 'Problems and development of the dry zone of West Africa', *Geogr. J.*, 127, pp. 187–204.

CLARKE, T. D., 1959, *Frontier America*, New York.

COLLINGWOOD, R. G., 1923, *Roman Britain*, London.

CORNISH, V., 1936, *Borderlands of language in Europe and their relation to the historic frontier of Christendom*, London.

CURZON OF KEDDLESTON, LORD, 1907, *Frontiers*, The Romanes Lecture, Oxford.

DAVIES, C. C., 1932, *The problem of the Northwest Frontier, 1890–1908*, Cambridge.

DENNIS, W. J., 1931, *Tacna and Arica*, New Haven.

EAST, W. G., 1937, 'The nature of political geography', *Politica*, 2, pp. 259–86.

EAST, W. G., 1962, *An historical geography of Europe*, 4th ed., revised, London.

EAST, W. G., and MOODIE, A. E., 1956, *The changing world*, London.

EAST, W. G., and SPATE, O. H. K., 1961, *The changing map of Asia*, 4th ed., London.

EAST. W. G., and WOOLDRIDGE, S. W., 1951, *The spirit and purpose of geography*, London.

FAWCETT, C. B., 1918, *Frontiers: A study in political geography*, London.

GOBLET, Y. M., 1955, *Political geography and the world map*, London.

HARRISON, J. A., 1953, *Japan's northern frontier*, Gainesville, Florida.

HERTSLET, SIR E., 1909, *Map of Africa by treaty*, H.M.S.O., London.

HOGBEN, S. J., 1929, *The Muhammedan emirates of Northern Nigeria*, London.

HÖHNEL, L. VON, 1894, *The discovery of Lakes Rudolph and Stefanie*, London.

HOLDICH, SIR T. H., 1916, *Political frontiers and boundary making*, London.

HOOSON, D. J. M., 1962, 'A new Soviet Heartland', *Geogr. J.* 128, pp. 19–29.

HUNTINGFORD, C. W. B., 1955, *The Galla of Ethiopia: The kingdom of Kafa and Janjero*, International African Institute, London.

KERR, D. G. G., 1961, *A historical atlas of Canada*, Toronto.

KRISTOFF, L. A. D., 1959, 'The nature of frontiers and boundaries', *Annals*, Association of American Geographers, 49, pp. 269–82.

LATTIMORE, O., 1940, *Inner Asian frontiers of China*, New York.

MARSHALL-CORNWALL, J. H., 1935, *Geographic disarmament: a study of regional demilitarization*, London.

MINISTÈRE DES COLONIES, 1910, *Documents scientifiques de la mission Tilho*, Paris.

PAULLIN, C. O., 1932, *Atlas of the historical geography of the United States*, Baltimore.

PEARCY, E., 1957, *World political geography*, London.

ROYAL GEOGRAPHICAL SOCIETY, 1951, 'Some definitions of the vocabulary of geography', *Geogr. J.*, 117, p. 459.

STAUDINGER, R.. 1889, *Im Herzen der Haussaland*, Berlin.

TURNER, F. J., 1953, *The frontier in American history*, 3rd impression, New York.

WEIGERT, H., and others, 1957, *Principles of political geography*, New York.

WILKINSON, H. R., 1955, 'Jugoslav Kosmet', *Transactions and Papers*, Institute of British Geographers, pp. 171–93.

WYMAN, W. D., and KROEBER, C. B., 1957, *Frontier in perspective*, Madison.

3

The evolution of boundaries

> The missionary, the conqueror, the farmer, and, of late,
> the engineer, have followed so closely in the traveller's
> footsteps that the world, in its remoter borders, has hardly
> been revealed before one must record its virtually complete
> political appropriation.   (Mackinder, 1904, p. 421)

Mackinder was speaking at the close of the most intensive period of boundary construction in the Earth's history; a period which had created a 'closed political system' including even barren tropical deserts and Antarctica. Except in the southern section of the Arabian peninsula, boundaries have replaced political frontiers. The last chapter indicated some of the ways by which the frontier is reduced in width; this chapter examines the way in which boundaries develop.

Boundary negotiations between states may originate once a conflict of interest develops, or appears imminent. This conflict of interest may involve territorial contact. For example there may be disputes about land ownership between governments or citizens of both states, and in this case the boundary will be developed subsequent to established cultural patterns of settlement, communication and administration. On the other hand the conflict may concern the territorial basis of planned state policies or ambitions. Many of the boundaries drawn in Africa, at the end of the nineteenth century, were antecedent to European occupation. They resulted from grandiose colonial schemes, such as France's desire to link her Mediterranean and Equatorial possessions. By examining both basic types of conflict it is possible to distinguish the detailed state motives involved.

Many boundaries are drawn in order to eliminate a potentially dangerous situation and to secure peace between the flanking states. Vattel regards boundary delimitation and demarcation as a useful cure for state disputes:

> ... pour éloigner tout sujet de discorde, toute occasion de querelle on doit marquer avec clarté et précision les limites des territoires.
> (Vattel, 1758, II, p. 137)

Many treaties defining boundaries begin by stating that the main aim is to secure good understanding between the signatories. The first article of the Sino-Russian Protocol of Chuguchak in 1864 provides an example.

> As a continuation of the treaty of Peking and for the promotion of the good understanding between the two Empires, at a general meeting in the city of Tarbagatai ... it was agreed to carry the boundary along the summits of mountains, along the great rivers and along the line of Chinese pickets existing at the present moment.
> (Inspectorate General of Customs, 1917, p. 144)

In 1897 there was the possibility of war between Britain and France over their conflicting colonial ambitions in the Niger Basin. The initiation of hostilities was expected to occur in the hinterland of Lagos, where British and French posts were interlocked. This dangerous situation was eliminated by the promulgation of a boundary, in 1898, separating the Lagos and Dahomey colonies. A decade later the Anglo-Russian Agreement, defining the limits of spheres of influence in Persia, ended an anxious period when the two countries seemed likely to engage in war.

Cases have also occurred when a state, facing defeat in war, has agreed to start boundary negotiations in order to preserve some measure of autonomy. The Guadalupe-Hidalgo treaty of 1848, which ended the Mexican-American war, resulted in Mexican territorial concessions to America, but did secure Mexican independence in the remaining territory. The desire to gain title to an area of strategic or economic potential has also served to encourage the onset of boundary negotiations. Britain, through negotiations with

Afghanistan, Persia, Tibet and China, sought to provide the Indian Empire with an easily defended boundary located in the peripheral mountain ranges, which Holdich regarded as the best 'natural frontier' in the world (Holdich, 1916, p. 148). Germany's proposals for boundary negotiations with Britain, concerning the hinterland of the Cameroons estuary, was intended to secure ownership of tropical areas which would provide valuable tropical crops, such as palm oil, and access to the navigable Benue, along which the interior of the colony could be most easily reached. The negotiations for this boundary were also encouraged by the simple economic fact that it proved impossible to encourage private firms to develop areas near the frontier between the two colonies. Such areas were regarded by the firms as being a poor financial risk, since political expediency might transfer their area of operation from one country to another, without adequate compensation (Rudin, 1938).

Finally, states may seek to create a boundary in order to regularize the administrative situation at the frontier; the presence of a no-man's-land between states facilitates escape by individuals from financial and juridicial responsibilities. It was noted in the last chapter that the frontiers were frequently occupied by brigands and refugees from justice. Britain and Germany in 1899 agreed to divide the neutral zone separating their Gold Coast and Togoland colonies by a boundary related to the main river in the area, in order to solve administrative problems which had arisen (Hertslet, 1909, p. 935).

Three aspects of boundary evolution are appropriate to geographical analysis – evolution in definition, evolution in position, and evolution in the state functions applied at the boundary. Examination of these three aspects will illuminate the two main lines of geographical research into boundaries – the influence of geographical factors on the location of the boundary, and the reciprocal influence of the boundary, once established, on the development of the landscape through which it is drawn.

Geographical knowledge is one of the fundamental factors which influence boundary location, and an indication of that knowledge is often contained in boundary definitions. Geometric boundaries in Africa usually meant that little reliable information was available about topography and drainage. Successive boundary definitions often record advances in exploration and cartography, as geometric boundaries are exchanged for lines coincident with rivers and relief features, or lines of cultural differentiation.

The way in which a boundary influences the development of a border landscape and the lives of its inhabitants is likely to be a function of the accuracy with which that boundary is defined and can be located, and the number and quality of state functions applied at the boundary. Often the most striking influences upon the border landscape and its inhabitants will result from changes in boundary position which transfer areas from one state to another. One example will serve at this point. After the second world war 2·8 million Germans moved out of former German territory east of the Oder-Neisse line, when it was transferred to Poland. The agricultural activities of the Polish immigrants in the transferred area, on both peasant and communal farms, have produced significant landscape changes (Wiskemann, 1956). In order to measure the geographical significance of the boundary, it is necessary to know the relationship which the original boundary bore to the landscape *at the time when the boundary was drawn*. This clearly involves the application of principles of historical geography, in order to discover the original correspondence between the boundary and the cultural patterns, such as the distribution of population groups, the location of economic activities, and the direction and volume of trade.

In outlining these avenues of research one begs the question, 'How can such material be accumulated?' Information about the boundary may be gathered by studying relevant documents, by analysing maps of the area and by carrying out fieldwork in the borderlands. The documentary material may be classified into three sections – correspondence between the negotiating powers, treaties agreed at the conclusion of negotiations, and publications by persons involved in the negotiation. The treaties and personal publications are generally readily available and it will be noticed that in many boundary studies reference is exclusively to these sources. The correspondence between states is only rarely published, and these documents must be consulted in archives, which generally will not allow examination of material less than fifty years old. However, such sources are invaluable since they alone record the detailed negotiations which led to the treaty. In the letters can be discovered the factors, geographical and otherwise, which have played an important part in producing the general location and detailed site of the boundary. Treaties will record only the agreed line. The study of Anglo-French correspondence during the negotiations concerned with the inter-Cameroons boundary (Prescott, 1963) revealed the following points that could not have been derived from the Milner-Simon Treaty of 1921 (Hertslet, 1923, pp. 275–8):

1. The position of the boundary in German Bornu resulted from the incorrect decoding of a British telegram in Lagos, in 1916.

2. As a result of the French refusal to rectify this error, Britain was able successfully to press for some areas to the south, which allowed reunification of the Holma, Zummu and Higi pagans, which had been separated by the Anglo-German boundary.

3. France was anxious to secure Garua, a port on the navigable Benue.

4. France was anxious to control the trade route from Douala to Garua, as an alternative to river access.

5. Britain set great store by the reunification of the former Emirate of Yola, which had been partitioned by the Anglo-German boundary, in such a way as to leave the capital – Yola – in Nigeria.

6. The use of inaccurate maps resulted in two disputes. The first, at the southern end of the line involving rich plantations, the other, in the north, relating to swamplands used for cotton cultivation and winter grazing.

7. The negotiations were conducted with regard to boundary arrangements being made in respect of other German colonies.

Boundary treaties are found in a wide variety of publications. Sir E. Hertslet has produced valuable collections of treaties dealing with the evolution of the political map of Europe and Africa, and many governments have published collections of treaties, some of which are listed at the end of this chapter. Unfortunately, many of the treaty series do not include the maps which form part of the treaty and, in such cases, these must be consulted in archives. For example, the terms of the Simla Convention of 1914 dealing with the Indian-Tibetan boundary are well known, but none of the published texts included the map on which the line was defined. Thus most students could make little progress in the study of this Agreement until the Government of India made the map available (Government of India, 1961). Boundary treaties will often include valuable information other than the definition of the boundary. Articles may be included to ensure certain rights of people living close to the boundary, or to specify government action to be taken after the Agreement has been ratified. Articles X and XI of the Anglo-German treaty of 1906 in respect of the boundary between Yola and Lake Chad was designed to safeguard the rights of borderland inhabitants.

Where the boundary is formed by rivers the population on both banks shall have equal rights of navigation and fishing. Wherever any land is transferred under this Agreement from the jurisdiction of one power to that of the other the occupiers of such land shall be allowed to elect freely on which side of the boundary they will reside, and they shall be allowed sufficient time to gather in any growing harvests, and to take the produce with them, together with all their property.

(Hertslet, 1909, p. 939)

The Anglo-French Agreement defining the boundary between the Gulf of Guinea and the Niger, in 1906, also protected the interests of the borderland inhabitants.

III   The villages situated in proximity to the boundary shall retain the right to arable and pasture lands, springs and watering places, which they have heretofore used, even in cases where such arable and pasture lands, springs and watering places are situated within the territory of one Power and the village within the territory of the other.

(Hertslet, 1909, p. 861)

Under the fifth and sixth articles of the Anglo-Tibetan Convention of 1904, Tibet undertook to keep roads from the boundary to Gyantse and Gartok free from obstructions and in a state of repair suited to the needs of trade, and to raze all fortifications along these routes which might impede communications (Inspector General of Customs, 1917, pp. 656–7).

During the period from 1890–1914 many boundaries were

delimited throughout Africa, Asia and South America, and commissions were sent to demarcate them. The leaders of many of these commissions published accounts of their experiences which afford valuable information about the problems faced and the reaction of the indigenous population to the boundaries. In many cases the leaders of both sections of the commission would record their work, and it is fruitful to compare the accounts in both languages. For example, Nugent (1914) and von Detzner (1913) published separate accounts of the demarcation of a section of the Anglo-German boundary, between Nigeria and Kamerun, and a careful consideration of the two accounts gives a much clearer picture of the problems overcome and the dislocation to the economic and political life of the tribes occupying the borderland, than does either account alone. Although personal accounts are not uniformly useful, most include maps which contain all the relevant geographical information available at that time. It must be stressed that boundary negotiations should be traced on the maps available to the negotiators, for many of the decisions would be inexplicable by reference to modern maps. For example, the Anglo-Russian Convention of 1825, in relation to the boundary between Alaska and British territory, stated in its fourth article that the boundary should 'follow the summits of the mountains situated parallel to the coast', providing that line shall not be more than thirty miles from the coast (Davidson, 1903, p. 81). Commentators have subsequently shown that such a boundary cannot be located (Davidson, 1903; Hinks, 1921). This boundary definition was accepted by the negotiators because their work was related to maps based on Vancouver's explorations of 1792–4, which were published in an atlas in 1798. Vancouver represented a range of mountains along the whole length of the Pacific coast of North America, varying from ten to twenty-four miles from the coast. Even in 1867, when Russia transferred Alaska to the United States, the official American charts were still based on Vancouver's maps.

The maps contained in the personal and official accounts of boundary commissioners often provide valuable information about the cultural landscape at the time the boundary was drawn, and therefore provide a standard against which subsequent change can be measured. In studying the effects of any boundary upon the cultural landscape, the geographer should use the largest scale maps available – those which show property boundaries are particularly useful.

Fieldwork is an indispensable source of information relating to boundary studies. The techniques of observation and local inquiry do not differ from fieldwork in other aspects of the subject, and should be directed towards the following points:

1. What is the condition of the boundary demarcation?

2. Does the boundary coincide with the published description?

3. Are there significant cultural landscape changes near the boundary?

4. How does the boundary affect the lives of the people living close to it?

5. Where are the major crossing points?

During fieldwork on part of the Lagos-Dahomey boundary, only three of the twenty blocks marking the section could be found. The three were all found near villages and none was complete, having in each case been used to sharpen cutlasses or axes. There were no significant changes in the cultural landscape within twenty miles of the boundary, and the lives of the people seemed unaffected by the boundary – some Nigerian farms were lying partly in Dahomey in accordance with the boundary provision quoted above (see above, p. 61). The two crossing points at Ijoun and Idiroko were thirty-two miles apart, and most of the border inhabitants crossed the boundary by uncontrolled paths. At times of tax collection, there was some movement across the boundary in order to escape responsibilities. During an interview with the Alaketu, who is a Yoruba chief in Dahomey, separated from the majority of his tribe in Nigeria, he said, 'We regard the boundary as separating the French and the English, not the Yoruba'. All this information was valuable in understanding the present condition and significance of the boundary, and could be obtained only by fieldwork.

Evolution in definition

Geographers have propounded several systems of boundary evolution. Brigham (1917) employed a threefold division – tribal, transitional and ideal. The tribal boundaries were primitive and were not defined in any document. Such divisions should be described as frontiers since they had a zonal quality, however clearly the last lines of defence were marked in the landscape. Brigham envisaged the transitional stage as being one when the boundary was likely to change its position, carrying the implication that the boundaries were finding a position where the forces from either side were neutralized. Finally, in the ideal stage the boundary became permanently fixed, and a gradual diminution of functions applied at the boundary reduced its significance as a landscape element. This altruistic concept of boundary evolution probably owed much to the world situation when it was published, and the ideas have not been further developed by subsequent workers.

Lapradelle (1928) distinguished three stages of boundary evolution – preparation, decision and execution. He emphasized the tentative nature of the first stage compared with those that follow by using *le trace*, which means 'outline' or 'sketch', instead of *la limite* meaning 'boundary'. Jones (1945) follows Lapradelle closely in suggesting four stages of boundary evolution – allocation, delimitation, demarcation and administration. Allocation refers to the political decision on the distribution of territory; delimitation involves the selection of a specific boundary site; demarcation concerns the marking of the boundary on the ground; and administration relates to the provisions for supervising the maintenance of the boundary. Nicholson (1954, p. 116) tried to marry the schemes of Jones and Brigham by carrying the process through from the tribal stage to the demarcated boundary. However, he admits that the only correlation between the first frontiers and the final boundaries in Canada were fortuitous, and that there was no continuous development. There seems to be no reason why his ideas should not apply where there is a continuous history of indigenous development. In cases of widespread colonization, as in America, Africa and Australia, the extent to which colonial boundaries are drawn within indigenous frontiers will depend on the extent to which the colonizing state considered existing political structures.

It must not be presumed that all boundaries have passed through the stages of allocation, delimitation and demarcation in an orderly sequence. In some cases the original allocating boundary has been demarcated with no intervening delimitation. In other cases there has been more than one delimitation before demarcation occurred. Finally there are many boundaries in the world which are still undemarcated. In the following discussion of boundary evolution the stages suggested by Lapradelle and Jones will be used.

Allocation

When a boundary was created in a frontier where the geographical facts were well known, and where the population density was moderate to heavy, it was sometimes possible to select the boundary site. In this case the stage of allocation would coincide with delimitation. In less well-known areas, often supporting a low population density, the first political division was by means of arbitrary boundaries of two main types. One type consists of straight lines connecting known points or coordinates; the other coincides with features of the physical landscape, which were often imperfectly known. Such boundaries were found in areas of colonial competition. The Portuguese-German Declaration of 1886, respecting the boundary between Angola and South West Africa, provides a good example.

> The boundary follows the course of the river Kenene (Cunene) from its mouth to the waterfalls which are formed south of the Hunbe by the Kenene breaking through the Serra Canna. From this point the boundary runs along the parallel of latitude to the river Kulingo (Okavango), then along the course of that river to the village of Andura (Andara) which is to remain in the German sphere of influence, and from thence in a straight line eastwards to the rapids of Catima (Katima) on the Zambezi.
> (Hertslet, 1909, p. 703)

The quotation shows how the boundary linked up known points by direct lines or stream courses. In this case no future problem arose, but in many cases exploration after the boundary had been defined showed that the description was impossible or that it bore no relation to the allocation of land intended. The classical problems of boundary interpretation associated with the Andean and Rocky Mountains between Chile and Argentina and between Alaska and Canada respectively illustrate this point, but it was not only physical features which were likely to confound subsequent boundary negotiations. The feelings of the Royal Niger Company about the sound basis for a boundary can be readily imagined from a letter to the Foreign Office which contains the following sentence:

> Meridians move about Africa like mountains. An error of a degree or even half a degree might cost England Kukawa, and therefore all Bornu.   (F.O.C.P. Confid. 6471, No. 254, R.N.C. to Foreign Office, 8th September 1893)

Until reliable determination of longitude was possible by time signals, calculations of longitude were likely to be inaccurate. The sequel to the letter quoted above is interesting. The Royal Niger Company objected to the definition of the terminal point of the Anglo-German boundary as the point where the fourteenth meridian east of Greenwich intersected the southern shore of Lake Chad. Accordingly the point was defined as the shore of Lake Chad 35 minutes east of Kukawa, capital of Bornu. This figure was based on Kiepert's *Deutscher Kolonial Atlas* which gave the longitude of Kukawa as 13°25′ east. There is reason to believe that this figure was based on the calculations of Vogel in 1853, which gave a result of 13°24′ east. In fact, the Demarcation Commission of 1903 found that the correct longitude of Kukawa was 13°33′ east, and thus the boundary terminated at 14°8′ east on the shore of Lake Chad.

An interesting sidelight on the initial allocation of territory and the subsequent problems of delimitation which might arise was thrown by Sir Claude Macdonald at a meeting of the Royal Geographical Society in 1914.

> In those days we just took a blue pencil and a rule and we put it down at Old Calabar and drew that line up to Yola. The following year I was sent to Berlin to endeavour to get from the German authorities some rectification of the blue line . . . and . . . my instructions were to grab as much as I could. I was provided with the only map – a naval chart with all the surroundings of the sea carefully marked out, but the rest was white . . . (except) . . . for the river Akpayoff which started near the Calabar river and meandered for 300 miles on the map. That was to be the boundary . . . (however) . . . there was no such river and the only river there was 3½ miles long.   (Nugent, 1914, p. 647)

Delimitation

The allocation of territory by arbitrary boundaries generally solved immediate territorial conflicts and allowed states to plan the development of colonies with security. The selection of a boundary site related to features of the physical and cultural landscapes was usually undertaken only when the borderland had an intrinsic economic value, or if the interests or antagonisms of the two states required the rigid application of state functions at a specific line. The retention of an original geometric boundary usually occurs when one or more of the following circumstances occur:

1. The borderland lacks economic and strategic value.

2. The states separated by the boundary are unable to agree to any alterations.

3. The boundary separates the colonial possessions of one power.

4. The separated states are more concerned with developing other parts of the territory than the borderlands.

An examination of a world political map will reveal that a high proportion of geometric boundaries are located in tropical deserts and Antarctica. The case of the Ethiopian-Somali boundary, through the Ogaden, illustrates the second situation. Considerable efforts by Italy and Ethiopia during the inter-war period ended unsuccessfully when Italy annexed Ethiopia. Under British administration during the war the problem was unimportant, but revived with the granting of the Somali Trusteeship to Italy after the second world war. Once again it proved impossible to agree to a more satisfactory line related to the needs of nomadic groups on both sides. Uniform British administration in South-West Africa and the Union of South Africa and in Kenya and Tanganyika after the first world war made it unnecessary to locate the boundaries separating these pairs of territories precisely. The last condition is illustrated by the case of Borgu – a former indigenous kingdom which was divided between British Nigeria and French Dahomey. Britain and France neglected this area once a boundary had been agreed in 1898 because they were much more concerned with developing more accessible and more valuable areas of their colonies. Once the two colonies became independent, the national governments pressed for delimitation in order to prevent tax evasion by border dwellers. The process of delimitation, at present uncompleted (1963), was started sixty-two years after the original boundary was drawn. This example under-lines the fact that delimitation may follow allocation at varying intervals and there may be successive delimitations before demarca-tion takes place.

Following Jones (1945), three types of boundary definition may be distinguished – complete definition, definition with power to deviate, and definition in principle. Complete definition provides a detailed description of the boundary site which ought to be capable of identification and demarcation by surveyors. Definition with power to deviate refers to those boundaries where the site is described in detail but where the demarcation commission may vary the line, for reasons of easy marking or administrative convenience. In such cases the maximum deviation is generally stated. In both types of definition the boundary may be defined in a variety of ways. One of the commonest methods is by a number of bearings and distances similar to those for a ship's course. The boundary between Nova Scotia and New Brunswick included a definition of this type.

> Then North 54 degrees 25 minutes East crossing the south end of Black Island 288 chains to the south angle of Trenholm Island, thence north 37 degrees East 85 chains and 82 links to a post, thence North 76 degrees East 46 chains and 20 links to the Portage.
>
> (Ganong, 1901, p. 369)

In using this method of definition it is important to avoid approxi-mate bearings and distances, to specify whether bearings are measured from true or magnetic North, and to provide alternative descriptions of the major turning points. Any errors made in measuring the line will accumulate and therefore it is valuable to have a check by independently identified turning points. When the country through which the boundary is drawn is imperfectly known, often the main turning points alone are recorded, and provision is made for some mutually acceptable line to be drawn between the points. The turning points may be clear physical features (or features which are thought to be clear), cultural features such as houses or road junctions, or astronomic co-ordinates. It has even been known for the boundary to be described with reference to letters on a defined map.

Boundaries have frequently been made to coincide with linear physical or cultural features. Linear cultural features such as roads, railways and fences are rarely used for international boundaries because of the administrative problems which arise, although they are often employed to define internal state boundaries. Physical features have long been used to define boundaries, a function which may seem appropriate from their map appearance. Many writers have drawn attention to the problems which have developed through referring to physical features in boundary descriptions as though they were points lacking area (Lapradelle, 1928; Boggs, 1939; Jones, 1945). The situation is most difficult when the boundary definition is made by negotiators who have no local knowledge of the area and who rely on inaccurate maps. For example the Commissioners delimiting the Anglo-French inter-Cameroons boundary in 1920 made their decisions in Paris on the basis of the Moissel map. This map covered Kamerun in a number of sheets on a scale of 1:300,000. A portion of the boundary north of the Benue was defined as follows:

> Thence a line southwestwards to the watershed between the basin of the Yedseram on the west and the basins of the Mudukwa and of the Benue on the east, thence this watershed to Mount Mulika.
>
> (Hertslet, 1923, p. 276)

When the definition was forwarded to the local British administrators, they replied in the following terms:

> there is no defined watershed common to the basins of the Mudukwa and the Yedseram, or the Mudukwa and the Benue. The region in question consists of isolated massifs. The Mudukwa and Yegoa rivers, affluents of Lake Chad, rise 40–50 miles from the nearest Benue tributary, with many transverse valleys between.
>
> (Africa West 1049, 7278, No. 83,
> Governor of Nigeria to Colonial Office, Feb. 11, 1922)

Loose contradictory terminology applied to physical features has probably created as many problems as ignorance about the distribution of features. With the exception of some precise landforms resulting from glacial erosion such as arrêtes, physical features have one or both of two characteristices which render them unsuitable for boundary definition. The characteristics are width and impermanence.

Definition in principle involves a statement of the basis of territorial partition and the result desired. Normally the territory is allocated on a basis of some human features of occupance. For example, in 1878 the Treaty of Berlin defined part of the boundary between Montenegro and Albania in these terms:

> It then coincides with the existing boundaries between the tribes of the Kuci-Drekalovici on one side, and the Kucka-Krajna, as well as the tribes of the Klementi and Grudi on the other, to the plain of Podgorica, from whence it proceeds towards Plavnica, leaving the Klementi, Grudi and Hoti tribes to Albania.
>
> (Hertslet, 1891, vol. 4, p. 2782)

In 1815, a Territorial Convention between Austria and Prussia defined the boundary by reference to many towns and cantons which were allocated to one side or the other of the line (Hertslet, 1875, vol. 3, p. 2062).

Demarcation

Demarcation involves the identification of the delimited line in the landscape, the construction of monuments or other visible features to mark the line, and the maintenance of the boundary markings. The instrument of delimitation usually contains one or more articles laying down the composition of the demarcation commission, the timetable of operations, and the distance by which the boundary might be varied from the delimited line. Demarcation does not always follow delimitation promptly. New boundary agreements may render them unnecessary, or matters of greater priority may make it impossible to spare survey teams for the work. Laws (1932) and Peake (1934) have described how the boundaries separating the former Belgian Congo from Northern Rhodesia and Tanganyika respectively remained undemarcated until copper and tin mining made demarcation essential if major disputes were to be avoided.

A demarcation commission may experience two types of problems. The first group arises from the interpretation of the boundary definition. The second group, which will not be considered here, includes problems associated with survey techniques in unfamiliar environments. Problems of demarcation which stem from the delimitation fall into four classes:

1. Ambiguous or imprecise terms.
2. Inaccurate descriptions including the use of false place-names.
3. The use of non-existent features.
4. Contradictory definitions.

Many writers have noted cases of ambiguous boundary definitions which created difficulties for the demarcation commission (Edwards, 1913; Cree, 1925; Clifford, 1936; Prescott, 1958 and 1963), but the example given here is taken from an interesting account by Hinks (1921), which considered several faulty delimitations in North and South America, Africa and Australia. The boundary between Peru and Bolivia north of Lake Titicaca was disputed by both states from their independence until arbitration by Argentina in 1909. The original boundary definition was based on inaccurate information and contained three statements which gave difficulty. First, the confluence of the Rivers Lanza and Tambopata – a turning point in the definition – was described as being north of the fourteenth parallel of south latitude, whereas it actually lay south of that line. Second, reference to the 'western source of the River Heath' was unfortunate since the country was too wild to allow its identification. Third, the stipulation that the boundary would pass 'westwards of the *barraca* of Illampu' after leaving the Madre de Dios River provoked a dispute concerning the meaning of *barraca* and the distance the boundary lay westward. *Barraca* could mean an estate or the principal house of the estate. Smith (1907) records the case of an inaccurate place-name creating difficulties on the boundary between Tanganyika and Kenya. The name Atorigini given to one of the mountains on the boundary was the Masai expression for 'I forget'!

The definition of a boundary by non-existent points is rarer than a contradictory definition. One example of the use of non-existent points was noted in the definition of the Nigerian regional boundary in the Niger Delta (Prescott, 1959).

The classical case of contradictory definition relates to the boundary between Chile and Argentina, promulgated in 1881. The conflict developed over the boundary section which was defined as 'the most elevated crests of said Cordillera that may divide the waters' (see Hinks, 1921, and Varela, 1899). In view of the attention which this case attracted, it is surprising to see the Indian Government lay so much emphasis on 'the watershed principle' in 1963 in its dispute with China.

In an account of this nature it would be inappropriate to consider the problems relating to survey techniques at length. It may be briefly noted that the work of boundary commissions was often arduous and protracted, especially when adverse weather restricted triangulation readings, or when the surveyors found it difficult to establish satisfactory stations, either owing to the thick vegetation or the extreme flatness of the landscape.

The geographer is interested in the appearance of the boundary in the landscape, and study of this is rewarding since the appearance will often give some clue to the significance of state functions applied there. The present contrast (1963) between the boundary separating the Soviet sector of Berlin from the other sectors of the city, and the boundary between the United States and Canada, underlines this point. In the same way the fieldworker can legitimately draw conclusions about the significance of a boundary where demarcation has been neglected, allowing cut lines to become choked with vegetation which makes boundary pillars difficult to find. Natural decay is not the only process by which boundaries become blurred. Clifford (1936) and Ryder (1925), working in Somalia and Turkey respectively, described how nomadic tribes destroyed boundary pillars within twenty-four hours of erection, in the belief that sovereignty was vested in the people rather than in the land. Jones (1945) has described in detail the ways in which a boundary can be marked.

Evolution in position

The fact that a political boundary may influence the evolution of the cultural landscape justifies the political geographer's interest in tracing the position of the boundary throughout its history. In order to evaluate the role of the boundary as a landscape builder it is essential to know for how long it occupied different positions, and the functions which were applied at the boundary during those periods. A second aspect of interest to the political geographer concerns the areas and populations changed from one administration to the other by shifts in boundary position. Clearly the changes are likely to be greatest when an international boundary is changed, and least in the case of an internal boundary marking the limits of an administrative area.

Before considering these points in greater detail, it is worthwhile to relate the scale of change in boundary position with evolution in boundary definition. The areas transferred by boundary changes usually decrease as the definition proceeds from the stages of allocation to demarcation. This point is well illustrated by the history of the Anglo-French boundary between the River Niger and Lake Chad. When the second allocating boundary, drawn in 1898, is compared with the first, dated 1890, it is noticed that the maximum movement of the boundary was ninety miles and that Britain had gained 14,800 square miles and lost 4,550 square miles. This situation was reversed by the delimitation of the boundary in 1904, when the maximum boundary movement was seventy miles and France gained 19,960 square miles. When this delimited boundary was demarcated in 1907 the Commission made only nine small changes, the largest involving only seventeen square miles.

Several studies have been made of the changes which have occurred when territory is transferred from one state to another by a change in the position of the boundary. The redistribution of population is a frequent result. Pallis (1925) reviewed the racial migrations in the Balkans during the period 1912–24, and concluded that these movements were the largest since those associated with the break-up of the Roman Empire. The movement of persons from territory ceded to neighbouring states formed a significant part of the migrations. For example, in 1913 the total Greek population, numbering 5,000, left the *qazas* of Jum'a-i-Bala, Melnik, Nevrokop and Stromitsa, when they were ceded to Bulgaria by the Treaty of

Bucharest. In 1914, approximately 100,000 Moslems left the portions of central and eastern Macedonia which had been ceded to the Balkan states by the peace treaty with Turkey, and settled in eastern Thrace and Anatolia. This scale of movement was exceeded after the second world war, when the Polish boundary moved westwards to the Oder-Neisse line, at the expense of Germany. Wiskemann (1956, p. 118) estimates that in 1946, 1,460,621 Germans left Polish-occupied territory and settled in British-occupied Germany, and that a further 600,000 moved into the Soviet sector. In the next three years a further 800,000 moved into the Soviet zone. By 1954 the number of Poles living in the Polish-occupied territory had risen from the pre-war figure of one million to seven millions (Wiskemann, 1956, p. 213). The changes in population structure in the former German areas were accompanied by alterations in the pattern of agriculture. All holdings over 100 hectares were confiscated and much of this land was redistributed to Polish peasants, as farms having an average size of twelve hectares. Altogether, 3·6 million hectares were distributed to 605,000 families. In addition, some collective farms were organized which bore a closer resemblance to some of the former German estates.

Economic changes resulting from boundary changes have also been studied by geographers, including Schlier (1959) and Weigend (1950). Schlier contrasts the spheres of influence of Berlin before and after the second world war, in respect of administration, services, food supplies, and employment. His maps show how Berlin's areas of influence in all respects have been truncated by the movement of international boundaries, and how links with the Federal Republic are restricted to a few well-defined roads, railways and air-corridors. Weigend (1950) examined the changes which occurred in that area of the South Tyrol which was transferred from Austria to Italy in 1919. He points to the striking proportional increase of Italians in the population, and makes some interesting comments on the economic changes. The fruit and wine producers of the transferred area continued to export their products to their traditional markets, which now lay across the boundary. Because the Italian producers were now competing on equal tariff terms it was necessary for the producers in South Tyrol to improve the quality of their products. Other farmers in the transferred area adjusted production to the requirements of the population of the Po plain, which had become their obvious market. The constant demand for seed potatoes and Swiss Brown cattle led to their import into, and production in, the transferred areas. Although the tourist trade suffered because of the transfer, this disadvantage was partially offset by the establishment of some industries including hydro-electricity generation and aluminium refining at Bolzano.

A review of the available studies of the effects of boundary changes suggests the general conclusion that the effects will be less severe when one or more of the following situations exists:

1. The altered boundary has existed for only a short time
2. Few state functions have been applied at the boundary
3. The groups formerly separated by the boundary have a cultural similarity
4. The economy of the transferred area was formerly oriented across the boundary
5. The economy of the transferred area is of a self-contained subsistence nature.

The transfer of the Juba strip to Italian Somaliland from the Protectorate of Kenya after World War I met the second, third and fifth conditions outlined above. Neither the Italian nor British Governments had rigorously applied state functions at the boundary, and the Somali groups from either side were free to cross the boundary to find pastures during their subsistence stock movements. For all these reasons the transfer took place smoothly without any dislocation to the lives of the borderland inhabitants.

The converse of this argument is that boundary changes are likely to be most severe in their effects upon the population and the landscape when the boundary has existed for a long time, when the population of the transferred area is ethnically dissimilar from the state in which they are incorporated, when the states applied many fiscal and security functions at the boundary, and finally when the economy of the transferred area was closely integrated with the core region of the state from which it is removed.

Evolution in function

The only function of a boundary is to mark the limits of authority or ownership. The nature of the boundary definition and the condition of the demarcated boundary will determine the effectiveness with which the boundary serves this function. In certain areas of desert or tropical forest, where international boundaries are located, it may often be difficult for a traveller or government official to know when he passes from one state to another. This has been one of the factors which has made the Sino-Indian border situation so difficult (1963). In less harsh environments this problem rarely exists.

Usually a state will find it convenient to carry out some of its functions at the boundaries. At points of entry, passport and customs regulations are supervised. These points of entry are likely to be at the boundary of land routes, and at the airport and seaport for other travellers. In these last two cases the checking is done at the first available point after the traveller has entered the area of the state's jurisdiction, which includes three or more miles of sea and an unspecified height of atmosphere. Boggs (1939) has listed state functions applied at the boundary, although he ascribes them to the boundary itself. No study has been traced of the order in which functions are exercised at the boundary and this may be because each situation is unique. Clearly friendly states will raise the fewest barriers to the circulation of goods and people, whereas hostile states may impose strict regulations on transit and trade, either continuously or at special periods. For example, it had become much more difficult in the past year (1962) to pass from East to West Berlin. When elections were held in Dahomey in 1961 the country's borders were closed for the period of polling. In similar fashion Guinea placed its boundary under strict supervision for one week while its currency was changed to a new form. When President Olympio of Togoland was assassinated, the government immediately closed the country's border with Ghana, because of the fear of increased disturbances. The imposition of tariffs at the boundary will vary with the economic condition and policy of the state. Growing unemployment in certain sectors of industry will often result in protection for that industry from similar imported commodities.

The subject of state functions has been neglected by political geographers and there are two possible lines of research which may prove useful. The first requires the correlation between the foreign policies of the state and the state functions applied at the boundary. The second analyses the variation in the role of the boundary as a landscape builder with the functions applied at the boundary. Both these subjects require considerable historical perspective and will probably prove most profitable in the case of states where there have been considerable changes in the direction and intensity of foreign policies.

To illustrate some of the points which have been made in this chapter it is proposed to consider the detailed evolution of the boundary between Mexico and the United States.

Evolution of the boundary between Mexico and the United States since 1847

A state of war legally came into existence between Mexico and the United States on May 13th 1846. In less than a year the American forces had made considerable advances and secured the Mexican Provinces of New Mexico, Upper and Lower California, Coahuila, Tamaulipas, Nuevo Leon and Chihuahua. Accordingly the American Government decided to appoint a Commissioner who would remain with the army and be ready to accept any opportunity for negotiating a satisfactory peace (Miller, 1937, p. 261). The conditions which the United States Government would find satisfactory were carefully laid down in a draft agreement which was given to the Commissioner; we are concerned here only with the territorial provisions.

At that time the *de jure* boundary between the two states was that promulgated in 1819 and coincident with the Sabine, Red and Arkansas rivers and latitude 42 degrees north. Under Article IV of the draft treaty, the United States sought a southward extension of the boundary to include all Texas, which had joined the Union in 1845, New Mexico, and Upper and Lower California.

The boundary line between the two Republics shall commence in the Gulf of Mexico three leagues from land opposite the mouth of the Rio Grande, from thence up the middle of that river to the point where it strikes the Southern line of New Mexico, thence westwardly along the Southern boundary of New Mexico, to the South Western corner of the same, thence Northward along the Western line of New Mexico until it intersects the first Branch of the river Gila, or if it should not intersect any branch of that river, then to the point on the line nearest to such branch and thence in a direct line to the same and down the middle of said branch of the said river until it empties into the Rio Colorado, thence down the middle of the Colorado and the middle of the Gulf of California to the Pacific Ocean.   (Miller, 1937, p. 265)

In addition to this territorial gain the United States sought to secure transit rights for American citizens and their goods across the Tehuantepec peninsula. The draft agreement represents the maximum concessions which America hoped to gain: the government indicated that they would be satisfied with less and outlined a series of payments which could be authorized to Mexico depending upon the territory and rights secured.

1. Up to $30 millions would be paid for Upper and Lower California and New Mexico, together with transit rights over the Tehuantepec peninsula.

2. Up to $25 millions would be paid either for the three Mexican provinces alone, or Upper California and New Mexico together with transit rights.

3. Up to $20 millions would be paid for Upper California and New Mexico.

If it proved impossible to secure Lower California, the conclusion of the boundary description would be altered to read as follows:

. . . to a point directly opposite the division line between Upper and Lower California; thence, due West, along the said line which runs north of the parallel of 32° and South of San Miguel to the Pacific Ocean.
(Miller, 1937, p. 263)

The intention of the boundary definition was clear, but it contained the seeds of disputes. Boggs (1939) has shown the difficulty of identifying 'the middle' of any river. Further the description assumed that there was no uncertainty about the position of the southern boundary of New Mexico. Lastly, considerable difficulty

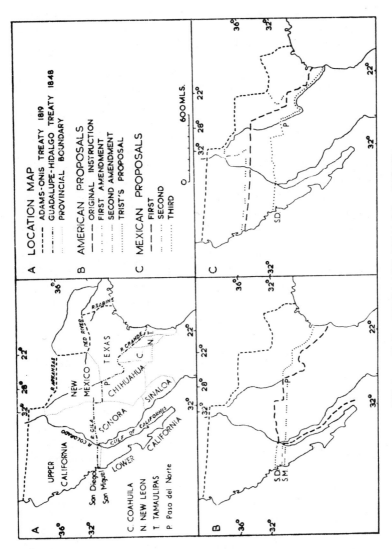

FIG. 2   THE GUADALUPE-HIDALGO TREATY

may have been attached in locating the point on the western boundary of New Mexico nearest to any tributary of the River Gila, and the actual situation might have involved a considerable northward extension of the boundary.

Second thoughts by the United States Government resulted in further choices being suggested to the Commissioner. In order to gain the Paso del Norte and the whole of the Gila Valley, which had been identified as a favourable route to the Pacific Ocean, it was suggested that the boundary should follow the Rio Grande to the thirty-second parallel of north latitude and along that latitude to the middle of the Gulf of California. This line could be extended across the Californian peninsula if Lower California could not be obtained, but it was essential that the Americans should have uninterrupted access through the Gulf of California and that San Diego be secured. This course was recommended since it would prevent any dispute about the southern boundary of New Mexico which, so far as America knew, had never been 'authoritatively and specifically determined' (Miller, 1937, p. 770).

At the first meetings between American and Mexican Commissioners the latter revealed their Government's proposals. No doubt, like the American draft, there were several possibilities. The most important point which emerged from the first exchange was that the Mexican Government laid down two conditions as *sine qua non* which prevented even the minimum American demands from providing a basis for discussion. First, the Mexicans required a neutral strip of territory adjacent to the north bank of the Rio Grande, in order to afford military protection against the United States and restrict the incidence of smuggling, which would reduce Mexico's revenue and injure their manufacturing industries. Second, Mexico required a land connexion between Lower California and Sonora around the head of the Gulf of California.

Instead of breaking off the negotiations, the American Commissioner exceeded his instructions and submitted a line which met the Mexican conditions to his Government, for their consideration. Historians have undoubtedly judged the Commissioner: geographers can be concerned only with the results of this action. The recommended boundary was defined as follows:

The boundary line between the two Republics shall commence at a point in the Gulf of Mexico, three leagues from Land, opposite to the middle of the Southern-most inlet into Corpus Christi Bay; thence, through the middle of said inlet, & through the middle of said bay, to the middle of the mouth of the Rio Nueces; thence up the middle of said river to the Southernmost extremity of Yoke Lake, or Lagunda de las Yuntas, where the said river leaves the said Lake, after running through the same; thence by a line due west to the middle of the Rio Puerco, and thence up the middle of said river to the parallel of latitude six geographical miles north of the Fort at the Paso del Norte on the Rio Bravo; thence due west, along the said parallel to the point where it intersects the western boundary of New Mexico; thence northwardly along the said boundary, until it first intersects a branch of the River Gila; (or if it should not intersect any branch of that river, then to the point on the said boundary nearest to the first branch thereof, and from that point in a direct line to such branch) thence down the middle of said branch & or the said River Gila, until it empties into the Rio Colorado, and down or up the middle of the Colorado, as the case may require, to the thirty third parallel of latitude; and thence due west along the said parallel, into the Pacific Ocean. And it is hereby agreed and stipulated, that the territory comprehended between the Rio Bravo and the above defined Boundary, from its commencement in the Gulf of Mexico up to the point where it crosses the said Rio Bravo, shall for ever remain a neutral ground between the two Republics, & shall not be settled upon by the citizens of either; no person shall be allowed hereafter to settle or establish himself within the said territory for any purpose or under any pretext whatever; and all contraventions of this prohibition may be treated by the Government of either Republic in the way prescribed by its laws respecting persons establishing themselves in defiance of its authority, within its own proper & exclusive territory.

(Miller, 1937, p. 288)

The form of this description implies that the neutral strip lay within Mexico, although the sense of the description is that it would be the responsibility of both Governments to restrict settlement there. It is not clear why, in order to give a land connexion between Lower California and Sonora, the boundary had to be drawn along the thirty-third parallel of north latitude, which would deny the United States access to San Diego and San Miguel. The 'parallel six geographical miles north of the fort at Paso del Norte on the Rio

Bravo' was coincident with the southern boundary of New Mexico shown on Disturnell's map, and thus avoided any dispute about the position of that provincial boundary.

There was no chance of America accepting this boundary since it would compromise Texan sovereignty and exclude America from the two main ports of Upper California and the Gulf of California. The American Commissioner was recalled before the resumption of hostilities, which was to force Mexico to sue for peace on American terms (Miller, 1937, p. 289–93). The American Commissioner continued to make history by ignoring his recall and remaining in Mexico to negotiate a treaty, although by then he lacked authority.

Before examining further negotiations, it may be recalled that up to this stage the process of boundary evolution had been normal. Both states had proposed lines which would allocate territory between the states to *their* greatest advantage. The descriptions revealed the generalized nature of geographical knowledge of the area, and were drawn in response to broad strategical motives. Mexico's proposal for a neutral zone is the transparent device of a weak state trying to limit its territorial concessions to a stronger neighbour.

The final round of negotiations began in December 1847. The Mexicans gave up the idea of a broad neutral zone, and instead sought to draw the boundary parallel to, and one league north of, the river. Further, they introduced a claim calling for part of the boundary to coincide with the summits of the Sierra de los Mimbres, which would have preserved the south-west quadrant of New Mexico. The Mexican Government did not give up its claims for a land connexion between Lower California and Sonora which would include San Diego.

It was only this last point which prevented rapid agreement, for it will be recalled that the American Commissioner had been instructed in the first draft to secure a boundary which was to be defined in the west as follows:

> . . . down the middle of the Colorado river and the Gulf of Mexico to a point opposite *the division line between Upper and Lower* California; then due west *along said line* which runs *north of the parallel of* 32° *and south of San Miguel* to the Pacific Ocean.   (Miller, 1937, p. 263)

The American Commissioner found himself in some difficulty for three reasons. First, some cartographic authorities showed San Miguel to be *south* of latitude 32 degrees north. Second, the Mexican Government, and other authorities, represented the political division between Upper and Lower California as being *north* of San Diego. Third, it was suspected (correctly) that the mouth of the Colorado River lay *south* of the thirty-second parallel.

Eventually, after several proposals and counter-proposals, the Commissioners agreed to a boundary which coincided with the original American draft except in the extreme west, where the boundary followed a direct line from the confluence of the Gila and Colorado Rivers to a point on the Pacific coast named Punta de Arena, which was south of San Diego (Miller, 1937, p. 325).

This suggestion was transmitted to both Governments, and not surprisingly the American Government decided to accept it although their agent lacked authority in the final negotiations. The treaty was endorsed by the American Senate, with certain amendments which did not relate to the territorial provisions. The fifth article defined the boundary in the following way:

> The Boundary line between the two Republics shall commence in the Gulf of Mexico, three leagues from land, opposite the mouth of the Rio Grande, otherwise called Rio Bravo del Norte, or opposite the mouth of its deepest branch, if it should have more than one branch emptying directly into the sea; from thence, up the middle of that river, following the deepest channel, where it has more than one, to the point where it strikes the southern boundary of New Mexico; thence, westwardly, along the whole southern boundary of New Mexico (which runs north of the town called Paso) to its western termination; thence, northward, along the western line of New Mexico, until it intersects the first branch of the river Gila; (or if it should not intersect any branch of that river, then, to the point on the said line nearest to such branch, and thence in a direct line to the same); thence down the middle of the said branch of the said river, until it empties into the Rio Colorado; thence, across the Rio Colorado, following the division line between Upper and Lower California, to the Pacific Ocean.
>
> The southern and western limits of New Mexico, mentioned in this Article, are those laid down in the Map, entitled 'Map of the United Mexican States, as organized and defined by various acts of the Congress

of said Republic, and constructed according to the best Authorities. Revised Edition. Published at New York in 1847 by J. Disturnell:' of which Map a Copy is added to this treaty, bearing the signatures and seals of the Undersigned Plenipotentiaries. And, in order to preclude all difficulty in tracing upon the ground the limit shall consist of a straight line, drawn from the middle of the Rio Gila, where it unites with the Colorado, to a point on the coast of the Pacific Ocean, distant one marine league due south of the southernmost point of the Port of San Diego, according to the plan of said port, made in the year 1782 by Don Juan Pantoja, second sailing master of the Spanish fleet, and published at Madrid in the year 1802, in the Atlas of the voyage of the schooners Sutil and Mexicana.   (Miller, 1937, pp. 213–5)

There are two points to notice. First, the description was similar to that originally proposed by America, and it continued to reflect the generalized topographical knowledge available about the area in question. Second, the definition hoped to avoid the two main points of controversy by specifying the maps which were authorities for fixing the southern and western boundaries of New Mexico and the terminal point on the Pacific Ocean. Subsequent events showed that controversy was not avoided.

In 1849 a Commission tried to determine the Pacific coast terminus of the boundary, which was

. . . one marine league due south of the southernmost point of the port of San Diego, according to the plan of the said port, made in the year 1782 by Don Juan Pontoja.   (Miller, 1937, p. 214)

The Commission found little correspondence between the map and the actual coastline. They did find one point near the port which appeared to coincide with the present coast. Accordingly they measured the distance on the map between this point and the southernmost point of the port. This distance was then laid off on the ground, and the marine league measured from there.

In 1852 the United States Government made financial provision for the Commission appointed to demarcate the southern and western boundary of New Mexico. The availability of the money depended upon the following condition being met:

> That no part of this appropriation shall be used or expended until it shall be made satisfactorily to appear . . . that the southern boundary of New Mexico is not established . . . farther north of the town called 'Paso' than the same is laid down in Disturnell's map, which is added to the treaty. (Miller, 1937, p. 369)

Now, according to the treaty map the latitude of El Paso was 32°15′ north, and the boundary intersected the Rio Grande eight miles north of the town, and extended 3½ degrees of longitude west of that river, which was shown to be in longitude 27°40′ west of Washington. The surveyors quickly found that the correct latitude of El Paso was 31°45′ north, and the boundary intersected the Rio Grande at longitude 29°40′ west of Washington. The Mexican members of the Commission pressed for a boundary starting on the Rio Grande at 32°22′ north and proceeding westwards for 1½ degrees of longitude. This means that they wished to accept the latitude of the boundary shown on the map, but correct the longitudinal error in the river position. For them the position of El Paso was unimportant providing it remained Mexican. However, the American Government insisted on following the map and using the position of El Paso as the datum from which measurements in the field would be made. The area between the two interpretations of the boundary was about 11,000 square miles.

Neither side was prepared to concede the area nor to compromise, and therefore new boundary negotiations were started in 1853. After extravagant proposals by both sides a new boundary definition crystallized out of the discussions. The new boundary followed the middle of the Rio Grande to latitude 31°47′ north, which it followed westwards for one hundred miles before turning due south to the parallel 31°20′ north. This parallel was followed westwards as far as longitude 111 degrees west of Greenwich. The boundary then followed a straight line to the Colorado River twenty English miles below its confluence with the River Gila, and then upstream along the middle of the Colorado to the line agreed in 1848 (Malloy, 1910, vol. 1, p. 1122). This line ceded about 24,000 square miles to the United States and secured for that state the entire catchment of the River Gila.

No problems were experienced in demarcating this second

allocating boundary between the Rio Grande and the Colorado River. The only problems associated with the boundary since 1853 have all been concerned with the Rio Grande, which proved to be most unstable in position in the section which marked the boundary. Changes in the river's course occurred gradually by accretion and suddenly by avulsion. The most enduring problem concerned El Chamizal, a tract of 630 acres opposite El Paso on the north bank of the river which forms the boundary. Mexico claimed that this area was south of the boundary in 1853, when the agreement came into force, but was transferred to the north bank of the river, when the course was suddenly changed in the floods of 1864. The two states could not solve the dispute, and arbitration by Canada in 1900 failed to produce an answer. The Canadian decision was that the boundary should follow the course of the river as it existed before the floods of 1864. It did not prove possible to establish this line through this territory to the satisfaction of both sides until 1964.

In 1884, the two states agreed that in future the boundary would coincide with the centre of the normal channel of the river and continue to follow changes in the river's course resulting from accretion. The boundary would follow the abandoned river course when changes resulted from avulsion. This meant that the area transferred from one bank to the other, when a meander neck was severed, locally known as *bancos*, would remain under the sovereignty of the original state (Malloy, 1910, vol. 1, p. 1159). In 1905 the governments agreed to minimize the difficulties resulting from avulsive river changes by exchanging all *bancos* other than those having an area of more than 617 acres or a population of two hundred. A permanent commission was responsible for this mutual exchange, which simplified boundary administration (see Paullin, 1932, p. 69 and plate 95D).

Further complications resulted from the fact that the Rio Grande is a valuable resource used by nationals of both states. To regularize the use of the water Mexico and America signed a Convention in 1906 to ensure equitable division. Under the terms of the Convention the United States Government contracted to deliver 60,000 acre feet to the head of a Mexican canal one mile below the point where the river became the international boundary. The United States would also be responsible for the distribution of water as far as Fort Quitman in Texas. In order to prevent damaging floods a dam was built in 1916 at Elephant Butte in Texas. This effectively stopped the flood waters derived from above the dam, but the reduction in the flow rate of the river resulted in the deposition of alluvium which had previously been scoured by floods. At El Paso the river bed was twelve feet higher in 1933 than in 1907. To remedy the situation the Governments agreed to construct a rectified canal from El Paso-Juarez to the mouth of the Box Canyon below Fort Quitman. The canal of eighty-eight miles shortened the river course by sixty-seven miles, and the increased gradient prevented alluvial accumulation. The canal was 590 feet wide and was aligned along the boundary axis, requiring both sides to exchange 3,500 acres. In addition to making the adjoining farmlands more secure from flood, the new canal increased the areas of land available for cultivation and simplified boundary maintenance and control.

This account of the evolution of the boundary between the United States and Mexico reveals four points. First, the American motives in concluding the initial boundary agreement were to secure at least the former Mexican territory of New Mexico and Upper California, and to end the war without the need to occupy all Mexico and maintain a military administration. Mexico agreed to negotiate in order to maintain sovereignty over the area south of the ceded portion.

Second, at no time was the boundary delimited. The Guadelupe-Hidalgo Treaty laid down a boundary which allocated territory between the two states, and this line was modified by the Gadsen Treaty, when the first boundary definition proved impossible to apply on the ground. In both cases the boundary was defined by imprecise physical features, and straight lines linking known points or coinciding with parallels of latitude or meridians. The descriptions reflected the generalized nature of existing knowledge about the area. Third, the demarcation of these allocating boundaries was hindered by the lack of correspondence between the maps named in the treaty and the actual landscape, and by the nature of the Rio Grande. Fourth, state controls over immigration and trade were applied as soon as the boundary could be identified.

References

BOGGS, S. W., 1939, *International boundaries*, New York.

BRIGHAM, A. P., 1919, 'Principles in the delimitation of boundaries', *Geogr. Rev.*, 7, pp. 201–19.

CLIFFORD, E. H. M., 1936, 'The British Somaliland-Ethiopia boundary', *Geogr. J.*, 87, pp. 289–337.

CREE, D., 1925, 'The Yugoslav-Hungarian boundary Commission', *Geogr. J.*, 65, pp. 89–112.

DAVIDSON, G., 1903, *The Alaska boundary*, San Francisco.

DETZNER, V. H., 1913, 'Die Nigerische Grenze von Kamerun zwischen Yola und dem Cross-Fluss', *Mitteilungen aus den deutschen Schutzgebeiten*, 26, pp. 317–38.

EDWARDS, H. A., 1913, 'Frontier work on the Bolivia-Brazil boundary', *Geogr. J.*, 42, pp. 113–28.

GANONG, W. F., 1901, 'The evolution of the boundaries of New Brunswick', *Trans. Roy. Soc.*, Canada (2), VII, pp. 139–449.

GOVERNMENT OF INDIA, 1960, *Atlas of the northern frontiers of India*, New Delhi.

HERTSLET, SIR E., 1875–91, *The map of Europe by Treaty*, 4 vols, London.

HERTSLET, SIR E., 1909, *Map of Africa by Treaty*, 3 vols, plus atlas, London.

HERTSLET, SIR E., 1923, *Commercial Treaties*, 29.

HINKS, A. R., 1921, 'Notes on the techniques of boundary delimitation', *Geogr. J.*, 58, pp. 417–43.

HOLDICH, T. H., 1916, *Political frontiers and boundary making*, London.

INSPECTORATE GENERAL OF CUSTOMS, 1917, *Treaties between China and Foreign States*, 2 vols, Shanghai.

JONES, S. B., 1945, *Boundary making: a handbook for statesmen*, Washington.

LAPRADELLE, P. DE, 1928, *La frontière*, Paris.

LAWS, J. B., 1932, 'A minor adjustment in the boundary between Tanganyika Territory and Ruanda', *Geogr. J.*, 80, pp. 244–7.

MALLOY, W. M., 1910, *Treaties, Conventions, international acts, protocols and agreements between the United States of America and other Powers, 1776–1909*, Washington.

MILLER, H., 1937, *Treaties and other Acts of the United States of America*, Vol. 5, Washington.

MOODIE, A. E., 1945, *The Italo-Jugoslav boundary*, London.

NICHOLSON, N. L., 1954, *The boundaries of Canada, its provinces and territories*, Department of Mines and Technical Surveys, Geographical Branch, Memoir 2, Ottawa.

NUGENT, W. V., 1914, 'The geographical results of the Nigeria-Kamerun Boundary Demarcation Commission', *Geogr. J.*, pp. 630–51.

PALLIS, A. A., 1925, 'Racial migrations in the Balkans during the years 1912–24', *Geogr. J.*, 66, pp. 315–31.

PAULLIN, C. O., 1932, *Atlas of the historical geography of the United States*, New York.

PEAKE, E. R. L., 1934, 'Northern Rhodesia-Belgian Congo boundary', *Geogr. J.*, 83, pp. 263–80.

PRESCOTT, J. R. V., 1958, 'Geographical problems associated with the delimitation and demarcation of the Nigeria-Kamerun boundary'. *Research Notes*, University College Ibadan, 12, pp. 1–14.

PRESCOTT, J. R. V., 1958, 'Nigeria's regional boundary problems', *Geogr. Rev.*, 49, pp. 485–504.

PRESCOTT, J. R. V., 1963, 'The evolution of the Anglo-French inter-Cameroons boundary', *Nigerian Geogr. J.*, 4, pp. 103–20.

RUDIN, H. R., 1938, *Germans in the Cameroons*, London.

RYDER, C. H. D., 1926, 'The demarcation of the Turco-Persian boundary in 1913–14', *Geogr. J.*, 66, pp. 227–42.

SCHLIER, O., 1959, 'Berlins Verflechtungen mit der Umwelt früher und heute', *Geographische Rundschau*, 11, Heft 4, pp. 125–51.

SMITH, G. E., 1907, 'From the Victoria Nyanza to Kilimanjaro', *Geogr. J.*, 29, pp. 249–72.

VARELA, L. V., 1899, *La République Argentine et le Chili: Histoire de la démarcation de leurs frontières (depuis 1843 jusqu'a 1899)*, 2 vols, Buenos Aires.

VATTELL, E. DE, 1758, *Le droit des gens ou principes de la loi naturelle appliqués à la conduite, et aux affaires des nations et des souverains*, Vol. 2, London.

WEIGEND, G. G., 1950, 'Effects of boundary changes in the South Tyrol', *Geogr. Rev.*, 40, pp. 364–75.

WISKEMANN, E., 1956, *Germany's eastern neighbours*, London.

4

Border landscapes

In the first chapter, it was stated that one of the principal interests in boundaries of any political geographer relates to the way in which a boundary or frontier influences both the landscape of which it is a part and the development of the policies of the states on either side. This view resulted from acceptance of the dictum, repeated by nearly all the authors reviewed, that it was meaningless to consider the boundary outside the context of the flanking state areas. Lapradelle termed this zone *le voisinage*, and 'border landscape' is suggested as an equivalent term. Political geographers are interested in boundaries because they mark the limits of political organization which varies over the Earth's surface. Variations in political systems are often accompanied by variations in regulations concerning economic activity and the movement of people, goods and ideas. The results of these variations are likely to be most clearly seen in the neighbourhood of the boundary, whether state functions are rigidly applied at the boundary, or whether the states combine to minimize the adverse effects of the boundary upon the border inhabitants. Few workers have selected this subject as the focus of their study, but many have included important references to it. Minghi (1963) did not suggest a separate group of such studies in his proposed classification of case studies, but included important papers by House (1959), Ullman (1939) and Nelson (1952) in categories dealing with the effects of boundary change and the characteristics of internal boundaries.

This chapter has been written because the author believes that students of political geography must concern themselves increasingly with the identification and description of political regions and the influence of political factors upon the cultural landscape. This is not to make any new conceptual suggestions, but rather to advocate a change of emphasis, and echoes Minghi's call for 'more attention to the normal situation in boundary research'.

There seems to be four aspects of this subject which fall within the province of the political geographer. First, there is the consideration of the boundary as an element of the cultural landscape. A boundary's physical existence results from the demarcation of the boundary and the construction of buildings, defences and systems of communications to give effect to state functions applied to it. The physical difference between an internal and international boundary is usually outstanding, but there are also important differences between different international boundaries. The suggestion has already been made that the appearance of any boundary in the landscape is a guide to the functions applied there, and the stringency with which they are applied.

Second, a geographer may wish to examine the extent to which variations in landscape and land-use on either side of a boundary can be explained by the proximity of two different political systems, and the regulations which they have developed. In this connexion it is important to distinguish such cases from those where variations in landscape and land-use result from the coincidence of the boundary with some linear physical feature such as a watershed which is also a climatic divide. Population distribution is one phenomenon related to land-use which may be partially explained by the nearness of the boundary. There are also cases where the existence of a boundary results in the duplication of transport, administrative and retail services.

The remaining two aspects are not directly concerned with the cultural landscape, but they may be conveniently considered here, since they may be the medium through which the boundary influences the cultural landscape. Third, there is the influence of the boundary's presence and operation upon the attitudes of the border inhabitants. Fourth, there is the influence which the boundary has upon the policies of the state, and in this connexion it may often be difficult to separate the effects of the nature of the boundary from those of the nature of the state beyond the boundary. Each of these aspects is considered in greater detail.

A boundary is usually demarcated only when the separated authorities believe this to be necessary. Some of the most important internal boundaries, which decide where persons may vote, at what level rates will be levied and the schools which children must attend, are never marked on the ground, but are shown on maps hanging in municipal and local government offices. In some cases, for reasons of pride local authorities in major cities will indicate when travellers along main routes are entering or leaving them. On the other hand nearly all international boundaries are marked on the ground in some way, simply because most states feel it is desirable that their limits should be understood by their neighbours.

The boundary may be identified in the landscape by two sets of features. First there is the indication of the boundary by means of markers, cut lines, fences and notices. Second there are various constructions designed to allow the smooth application of state functions at or near the boundary. Many travellers will be familiar with customs posts located near barriers across main roads, and stations built on the boundary to allow passengers to be subjected to custom and immigration regulations. It should also be noted that international airports and seaports and coastal defences are types of border landscapes.

Since nearly all international boundaries are demarcated in some way, it is possible to draw from the nature of the demarcation certain inferences about the nature of state functions and the relationship between the separated states. The following paragraphs indicate the type of conclusion which may be reached in the three most common situations, although the reader is reminded that boundaries tend to be unique.

If an international boundary is not demarcated there are three probable explanations. First, the states concerned may not feel that demarcation is necessary, or of high financial priority. Many of the international colonial boundaries were not demarcated because of the expense involved and the improved relations between the colonial powers. Second, boundaries may not be demarcated because the exact position of the boundary is disputed, due to some ambiguity in the definition of the boundary. This cause retarded the demarcation of many South American boundaries and currently continues to prevent any demarcation of the boundary between Somalia and Ethiopia. When a boundary is disputed, however, it will often be found that military and police installations are located in the border area in order to preserve rival claims. One obvious reason for not demarcating an international boundary may be found in the unfavourable nature of some environments. Where international boundaries lie within hot deserts or high mountain ranges demarcation is often regarded as unnecessary on the grounds of security and impossible on the grounds of finance. However such views may change as mineral exploration raises the possibility of discovering worthwhile deposits in deserts, and improved military techniques and changed military power reduce the defensive value of mountain ranges. It seems likely that both Algeria and India will insist on boundary demarcation when their disputes with Morocco and China respectively are settled. Where a boundary is drawn within an unfavourable environment it will often be found that both the states establish their police and customs posts on the edge of the area. This means that the intervening area is not under direct and continuous control.

If the boundary is demarcated, two general situations can be distinguished. The first occurs when the demarcation is maintained, and the second when it is neglected.

Looking first at the case where the demarcation is maintained, two extreme conditions can be described which will limit a host of variations and combinations between.

At one end of the scale there are the boundaries between allies, such as Canada and the United States of America. Here the boundary vistas are carefully cut and the boundary monuments kept in good repair even on the more remote western borders. This is largely for reasons of administrative convenience, and not to restrict circulation. Structures to allow the application of state functions are located at the important recognized crossing points. Along such boundaries there is often an absence of permanent fortifications. At the opposite end of the scale there are those boundaries between unfriendly states where the boundary demarcation is maintained in order to prevent circulation and to simplify defence. The boundary in such cases is often marked by an obstacle such as a fence or a wall, and guard posts are located at regular intervals along the entire length. A strip of land adjacent to the boundary may be cleared to make observation easier and illegal boundary crossing more difficult. The civilian population is often evacuated from such a border. The crossing points on these boundaries are few and heavily guarded. These features may all be seen on some sections of the boundary between East and West Germany, especially in Berlin, and the land boundaries of Israel with its Arab neighbours.

Between these two extremes may be found a wide variety of boundary forms, and there may be significant variations along any boundary. Boundary form is also likely to vary with changing circumstances. The steady deterioration of relations between Ghana and Togoland resulted in clearer boundary demarcation and increased boundary supervision. Since the assassination of President Olympio there has been some reduction in the stringent application of state functions at the boundary.

When a boundary has been demarcated and that demarcation has not been maintained, the political geographer may find this a useful pointer to changed political situations. In some cases colonial powers at the height of their competition carefully marked their boundaries, but once the period of competition gave way to a period of development with its attendant concentration on internal affairs, the border areas were often neglected either for reasons of priority or to avoid incidents. Boundary vistas became overgrown, and people, animals and vegetation destroyed boundary pillars. The re-establishment of these boundaries by the independent successors to the colonial states often causes friction and gives rise to territorial disputes.

Both international and internal boundaries may mark changes in the landscape and economic activity, which result from the separate areas being subject to different regulations. It follows, however, that the greatest variations occur between different countries, and the differences associated with international boundaries tend to be more striking than those associated with internal boundaries. Since only a few studies have been made into this aspect of boundary research it seems worthwhile to record them, and to consider separately those related to internal and international boundaries.

Platt and Bücking-Spitta (1958) published an interesting descriptive account of the Dutch-German boundary, which passed through areas of agriculture, industry and mining. In examining agricultural landscapes and production in three different areas, Platt found no significant differences on opposite sides of the boundary. The three areas were the polder country near the North Sea, the moor-edge settlements of Bellingwolde and Wymeer, and the flood plain and diluvial terraces of the River Rhine. Not only were the areas used by farms of similar size, divided into similar field patterns producing approximately the same proportions of various crops, but the building styles were also similar on both sides. The textile industry north of the Rhine, including Enschede and Gronau, was originally established as an 'international industry' whose operation was unaffected before the first world war by the presence of the boundary. Since then the two areas have tended to become more national in character but there is still some movement of workers across the boundary. At the time of the study (1953) conditions were more satisfactory in Holland and there was accordingly a greater volume of movement of Germans into Holland than Dutch citizens into Germany. In the small coalfield around Kerkrade, Platt found no variations in distribution, method of production and output which could not be explained by the differing physical circumstances of the coal reserves on each side.

Platt then examined the political and economic organization of the border areas, and again found that there were similar forms on both sides of the boundary. His final conclusion was interesting, and seems to provide an important principle.

The preceding chapters have dealt with the characteristics of the border areas. Landscape and occupance have been found similar on opposite sides. The boundary is not natural and does not separate different uniform regions. It could be pushed east or west without changing the appearance of things in general on opposite sides.

. . . although the forms of areal organization may be similar on opposite sides of the boundary, the organizations themselves, the units of organization, political, economic and social, as they have developed through years of human activity, are generally separate. A shift of the boundary in either direction disturbs the organization in units small and

large on both sides, and generally does damage which can only slowly
if ever be repaired.   (Platt and Bücking-Spitta, 1958, p. 85)

Platt's conclusions indicate quite clearly that although the boundary
separates areas with almost identical landscapes and systems of
organization there remain vital intangible differences of political
attitude and social custom. These are aspects which a geographer
finds difficult to measure, and about which only general ideas could
be formulated even after a long residence in the borderlands.

This descriptive study was principally concerned with the present,
unlike that made by Daveau (1959) which considered the Franco-
Swiss borderland in the Jura over several centuries. This admirable
study, which does not seem to have attracted the attention it deserves,
shows clearly how the influence of the boundary on the borderlands
will vary as political and geographical circumstances change. It
would be surprising if this was not the case, but it is valuable to have
such a clear demonstration. Daveau shows how the presence of the
boundary has influenced the development of agriculture, forestry
and industry since it was established.

The area considered lies west of Lake Neuchâtel, and the principal
agricultural activity was the raising of stock and the preparation of
dairy products, especially cheese. During the early eighteenth century
there was a considerable measure of interpenetration of pasture
lands, and Daveau calculated that Swiss farmers owned 400 hectares
of French land while French farmers owned 1,000 hectares in
Switzerland. The areas of greatest French colonization were in the
neighbourhood of les Verrières and la Brevine, which carried a low
density of Swiss. After the Reformation, many Swiss and French
farmers sold their land across the boundary because of the rise of
national consciousness, the complex regulations covering alien land-
ownership, and the problem of maintaining the property when the
countries were at war. During the nineteenth century further
changes took place. There was a withdrawal of French population
from the upper pastures of the French border and a concentration
in the valleys. This coincided with a considerable increase in the
Swiss herds, many of which were accommodated on leased French
pastures. At the same time there was a greater concentration of beef

and veal production at the expense of dairy products, which were now manufactured mainly in the valleys on both sides of the border. The extension of Swiss control over French border areas was increased by the fall of the French franc compared with Swiss currency during the first world war. However, the threats of further falls in the value of the French franc encouraged Swiss farmers to lease land rather than buy it outright. They were in the fortunate position of being able to fatten the cattle cheaply in France and sell the meat at the higher Swiss rates in Switzerland. The French villages in the valleys do not benefit from the Swiss occupation of the uplands since the herdsmen generally bring all their provisions from Switzerland. Conventions of 1882 and 1938 allow free circulation of agricultural products within a zone ten kilometres wide on each side of the boundary. The actual wording of the relevant sections allows a number of interpretations, and variations are found between the arrangements in the Department of Doubs and the Canton of Vaud. Some landscape differences are noted where the boundary crosses a valley. One air photograph clearly shows the contrast at the boundary between the small strip fields of Amont in France and the summer pastures of Carroz in Switzerland, even though the physical character of the landscape on both sides is the same.

Dans plusieurs forêts de ces montagnes, la ligne de demarcation entre la France et la Suisse est sensiblement tracée par la mauvaise exploitation de nos bois, et le voyageur qui se rappellera ce fait pourra, sans guide et sans garde, reconnaître la limite en quelques endroits et toucher, avec assurance, d'une main un sapin suisse et de l'autre un sapin français. (le Quinio, quoted in Daveau, 1959, p. 386)

This quotation shows that even in the eighteenth century landscape differences could be noticed in respect of the exploitation of forests. Daveau shows that this situation exists today, although for different reasons. At first the forest was regarded as a useful buffer zone between the Swiss and French, and restrictions were imposed upon the cutting of wood. In the period before 1750 there were many cases of wood in French territory being illegally cut by Swiss citizens. In the post-1750 period the situation was reversed; French depredations in Swiss forests were the general rule and there were minor wars as the Swiss attempted to protect their territory. The conflicts eventually stopped as the areas became more densely populated and customs patrols became more active on each side. In 1882 under a boundary convention customs officers were given authority to pursue illegal woodcutters across the boundary, and the duty-free transport of 15,000 tons of firewood was allowed within a zone ten kilometres wide on each side of the boundary. In 1938 this figure was reduced to about 9,000 tons. Once again as in the case of pasturage the decline of the French franc in relation to the Swiss franc allowed Swiss citizens to gain an advantage. More and more forest in the French border has been bought by Swiss who have then realized quick profits by wholesale cutting and clearing, without any plans for reafforestation. The denuded lands are converted to pasture which is then sold or leased to Swiss cattle farmers. This practice produces striking landscape differences on opposite sides of the boundary. One air photograph, included by Daveau, shows how the forests on the French side of the boundary have been almost completely cleared while those on the Swiss side remain in a well-kept condition (Daveau, 1959, plate 11).

The analysis of farming and forestry in the borderland led Daveau to conclude that the economic boundary lies in Switzerland's favour, to the west of the political boundary. The reciprocity written into the border conventions is meaningless as long as the French franc stands at an unfavourable rate to the Swiss franc. This is a clear warning to geographers not to accept written guarantees in boundary treaties at face value; their application must be tested.

Daveau also examined the influence exerted by the boundary upon the watchmaking industry of the Franco-Swiss Jura. The industry began in Switzerland, and the first French factory was at Besançon. Before 1834 the French Government tried to protect the French industry from Swiss competition by high tariffs and the suppression of smuggling – which was a profitable occupation for French and Swiss citizens alike. In 1826 it was decreed that all French watchmakers must have their premises at least seven kilometres from the boundary. The duty on Swiss watches was reduced after 1834 to

4 per cent *ad valorem* in 1836. This low rate did not make smuggling worthwhile and the activity declined rapidly, but by 1842 the smugglers realized that it was worthwhile to take French watches to Switzerland and then re-import them as Swiss watches. This flourishing trade continued for some time.

In the last years of the nineteenth century a tariff war between France and Switzerland resulted in a distinct rupture between the two industries. This helped certain sections of both industries. The Swiss apparently captured more of the market in small watches. In France certain workers who had specialized in making escapements could no longer export their product to Switzerland, and they turned to the manufacture of complete watches. Further, France began to deal directly with overseas markets which had previously been supplied by Swiss merchants who bought from French producers. We can see then that the regulations laid down by the governments affected the location of the industry on the French side and the traffic in watches, and caused variations in the type of production.

These studies by Platt and Daveau have shown that international boundaries may lie through identical cultural landscapes or mark significant changes in land-use and economic activity. Both would agree that, however similar the borderlands, the two sides have a human distinctiveness which is difficult to measure, but which is nevertheless real to people living in the borderland. Daveau has shown how important it is for political geographers to have an awareness of currency variations in explaining changes in the significance of the boundary over a long period.

This view is confirmed by the experience of Sevrin (1949) who studied trans-boundary population movements on the Franco-Belgian borderland. In 1929 there were 10,219 Belgians working in the French borderland and this figure declined to 2,757 in 1946 as a result of the war and the attendant decline in the value of the franc. By 1947 the number had increased to 8,810 as there was an upsurge in textile production, and as measures were implemented to maintain the exchange value of the French franc.

On the influence of internal boundaries there are three papers of particular relevance. Ullman and Rose considered the influence of selected federal boundaries in America and Australia respectively, while Nelson examined the significance of the internal boundaries of part of California in relation to understanding the development of its urban landscape.

Ullman's study of the eastern Rhode Island-Massachusetts boundary revealed that the boundary, which was accordant in situation but discordant in site, did influence the establishment of industries south of the Fall River. The industries were located in Rhode Island to gain tax concessions, but the tenements for the workers were located in Massachusetts, so that the workers could continue to enjoy the superior social and cultural amenities offered by that state. It was noticed that the boundary became zonal in some respects because water, gas and electricity services were common to sections of both states, and because some private properties spanned the boundary.

Rose (1955) studied the eastern section of the boundiary between Queensland and New South Wales, and discovered that it coincided with some landscape differences which had arisen since the boundary was delimited, and which could not be explained in terms of environmental differences. One case concerns the establishment of intensive orcharding on the Tableland inside Queensland, whereas across the boundary in New South Wales ranching remains the staple industry. The Queensland orchards developed as a result of the deliberate settlement policy of the Queensland Government after the first world war. The industry was further encouraged by the provision of efficient transport and marketing services. Rose also noted that the influence of the boundary upon the landscape is likely to become blurred as a result of the extension of road services, and the unification of electricity and gas services.

Nelson (1952) examined the boundaries of the Vernon area of California, to assess their contribution to an understanding 'of the areal distribution and functioning association' of various elements of the urban landscape. He plotted the distribution of residential, commercial, public, industrial and transportational land-use, and found that the boundary of Vernon coincided with significant landscape differences. There was a remarkable concentration of land devoted to industry and transport within Vernon, almost to the complete exclusion of the other three categories. It also emerged that other boundaries in the Vernon area did not coincide with similar distinctions in land-use. This suggests that Nelson was fortunate in his selection of Vernon as a case study, and that the technique he used will be valuable only in a few instances. While it may be true that a simple land-use analysis will rarely show significant correlations with political boundaries, if Nelson's technique is carried a stage further and *quality* of land-use is studied, it should have much wider application. For example instead of distinguishing residential and other types of land-use, it will be necessary to examine the residential category in greater detail, collecting information about house-types and rateable values. In a cosmopolitan city it may be of significance to record the nationality of house occupants or owners.

A further technique useful in such studies has been suggested by Mackay (1958), who has applied Dodd's interactance hypothesis to boundaries. By comparing the value of actual and computed interactance between cities or areas separated by a political boundary, Mackay suggests that it will be possible to obtain a measure of boundary interference. This would be useful in assessing the significance of individual boundaries, and comparing the significance of two or more boundaries. These studies would be limited to areas for which detailed statistics are available, and Mackay warns that factors other than the boundary may produce differences between computed and actual interactance. It would also seem worthwhile to investigate the extent to which the model prepared by Dodd is applicable to boundary studies in areas dissimilar to North America in political, economic and social development.

The studies reviewed in this section suggested that internal boundaries do influence the development of the cultural landscapes in many ways, and that the analysis of these relationships is a worthwhile, though neglected, aspect of political geography, which could provide valuable information for those interested in economic and urban geography. The influence of the internal boundaries is less spectacular than that of international boundaries, and will be revealed only by careful research. Before leaving this subject it is necessary to counsel care in the use of statistics in demonstrating the influence of the boundary upon the cultural landscape. Federal boundaries always form the basic framework for statistical divisions, which may also coincide with some sections of internal boundaries. It is therefore not surprising that in many cases the political boundary will appear to separate areas with different population densities and *per capita* agricultural outputs. Such differences may only be apparent, and field examination may show that differences in population density and intensity of activity do not coincide with the political boundary.

It was suggested in the introduction to this chapter that a boundary may exert some influence upon the attitudes of persons living in the borderland and on the policies of states separated by the boundary. The studies have not yet been made which would justify or reject this concept, and accordingly the following views must be regarded as tentative. If the influence of the boundary upon the attitudes of border dwellers is examined first, three points can be made. First, no one can doubt that 'frontiersman' denotes a person with a particular kind of philosophy and character: this point was most convincingly made by Turner and has been repeated by others such as Kristoff (1959). Since any international borderland bears some relationship with a frontier, we can expect the boundary to have some measure of influence. The influence is likely to be exerted through the opportunities which the presence of the boundary offers for economic gain, the inconveniences presented by the boundary to everyday living, and a greater awareness of the security needs of the state. One would expect the Belgians living on the German border to have a different awareness of the need for military preparedness from the Belgians living in the interior of the country and along the French border. The differences between the security viewpoints of the border and core dwellers is likely to be greater in countries larger than Belgium. The great difficulty is to measure the extent to which the attitude of borderland dwellers is distinctively influenced by the presence of the boundary. In some cases the borderland may give support to a specific political party which will express clear views on questions of tariffs, boundary and security arrangements. In other cases referenda relating to the boundary may be informative. This is obviously true when the issue concerns the movement of the boundary, as certain referenda did in Europe after World War I, but is also true when it concerns altering the functions of the boundary, as in the Australian referendum on the formation of a federation. Some details of this case are presented at the end of this chapter. Probably the most successful method of measuring the borderland attitudes is by field work over a long period.

It is similarly difficult to be certain that the nature of a particular boundary has influenced state policies, since such material is frequently contained in inaccessible archives. Further it will not always be easy, nor profitable, to distinguish the influence of the boundary from the influence of the state with which the boundary is drawn. The contemporary international scene suggests at least two cases where policies may result from the nature of the boundary. In the second half of 1963 the Australian Government began to demarcate more clearly the boundary separating their New Guinea territories from West Irian. This policy probably results partly from the unsatisfactory condition of this longitudinal boundary, and also from the territorial friction between Indonesia and Malaysia. Had the Dutch remained in control of West Irian it is unlikely that it would have been considered worthwhile spending funds on boundary demarcation. Second, there is the example of India, which in the years since independence has neglected her apparently secure Himalayan border in order to concentrate upon the development of the remainder of the country and the security of her Pakistan border. Even the re-establishment of Chinese influence in Tibet did not alter this policy, which was only ended when Chinese allegedly invaded Indian territory in the Himalayas. Apart from examples and inferences of this kind, it seems likely that more concrete examples will have to be derived from historical studies in political geography using first-hand material in archives.

There is of course no shortage of examples of boundary disputes which indicate the influence of alleged mal-functioning or mis-alignment of the boundary upon state policies. Such cases have already been considered in another chapter.

The only studies of border landscapes by the author were made in Africa, and in order to prevent this book from acquiring an over-powering African flavour the case study to illustrate this chapter is taken from a research project by an Australian student. Logan (1963) studied the influence of selected internal boundaries in south-west Victoria in preparing a dissertation for a degree of Bachelor of Arts, in the University of Melbourne.

The significance of the federal and some internal boundaries in south-western Victoria

Before 1901 Victoria and South Australia were individual colonies and the boundary between them was similar in many respects to an international boundary. However, their similarities of origin and administration reduced the significance of the boundary as a landscape element. For example the Victorian Government adopted a policy of protection for many domestic industries, but this policy had little influence in the borderland with South Australia because the two colonies produced similar foodstuffs and had similar deficiencies. This policy was more significant in the borderland with New South Wales. Nor did the boundary act as an obstacle to population movement. During the expansion of the gold industry in Victoria many workers came from South Australia, and it was from that state that many farmers came when the Wimmera was developed at the end of the last century. During the economic depressions at the end of the last century many citizens of Melbourne migrated to areas which included rural South Australia. One of the most striking influences of the boundary was upon the alignment of transport routes. The extension of the Victorian broad-gauge system into Mount Gambier after 1885 was the first significant development of a trans-boundary communication network. Logan was satisfied after analysis that the colonial boundary had little effect upon the border landscape or the circulation of people and goods.

> Nevertheless, the customs and migration regulations and the differences in transport systems and freight rates applied at the boundary of each colony exerted sufficient divisional influence to become regarded, particularly by the metropolitan, commercial and industrial entrepreneurs, as a hindrance to the progress of the continent.
>
> (Logan, 1963, p. 64)

It therefore seemed worthwhile to examine the influence of the boundary, if any, upon the attitude of the border dwellers to the proposed Federation. Two views are held by historians on this matter. Parker (1949) holds the opinion that most voters judged federation in terms of regional economic interest.

> Federation by establishing a customs union, and perhaps by setting limits to railway competition and ensuring unhampered transport on the Murray system which flows through three colonies, is inevitably attractive to border residents and repulsive to the urban interests which rely on discriminatory legislation in order to participate in an otherwise uneconomic commerce.　　　　　　　　　　　　(Parker, 1949, p. 1)

Blainey (1949) on the other hand believes that there is a considerable variation within the voting patterns of the borderlands, suggesting that this influence is not uniform. When the referendum statistics were plotted on a map the result tended to support Parker's concept. In south-western Victoria the border constituencies of Lowan, Normanby and Portland recorded a higher proportion of affirmative votes than the state average (82 per cent) and the metropolitan vote (77 per cent). In the Victoria and Albert constituencies of south-eastern South Australia 78 per cent of the voters were in favour of federation compared with the state average of 67 per cent and the metropolitan figure of 55 per cent. While proximity to the boundary is not the only factor involved, the figures are suggestive. Neglect of the more remote state areas by the metropolitan administrations may also have been responsible for the larger vote. There were variations within the border however, and Blainey's position can be understood. Some electorates which lay close to the boundary, but which had no trans-boundary contacts, returned lower percentages of affirmative votes. Port Macdonnell, which lies only fifteen miles within South Australia, is an example of this type of electorate.

When the Federation was formed in 1901, the reduction in state powers reduced some of the state functions applied at the boundary and its divisive character was theoretically reduced, although it has already been noted that the boundary had little effect on circulation or landscape. Logan tested the applicability of the interactance hypothesis suggested by Mackay (1958) in respect of telephone calls between selected centres in Victoria and South Australia. The analysis by this method indicated that the boundary was not an interruptive factor, for the actual level of telephone contact was in excess of the calculated level in all except one case. Logan suggests that the formula would be more meaningful if the distance between the centres was taken to be that by existing transport routes. It would also be helpful if the difficulty of travelling from one centre to another could be assessed. Time taken by the most readily available means of transport might be the most satisfactory measurement.

Since 1901 certain landscape differences have developed along the boundary as a consequence of the different policies adopted by Victoria and South Australia. Owing to inaccurate delimitation, Victoria gained a narrow strip of land which South Australia subsequently sought to recover through court action. In order to justify their case for retaining the territory, the Victorian Government used some of the land for the establishment of soldier settlement estates, which contrast with the pastoral areas and forest reserves in South Australia. The shortage of suitable supplies of timber in South Australia encouraged the planting of softwood plantations (*Pinus radiata*). Five of the six plantations in existence terminate at the boundary and form a distinct contrast with the eucalyptus woodlands in Victoria.

Minghi (1963a) suggested that an analysis of the preference for competing television or radio stations might be the means of assessing political attachments in the border zone. Logan attempted to follow this lead by analysing sales statistics of two newspapers, the Melbourne *Sun* and the Adelaide *Advertiser*, in the border area. While recognizing that there are complicating factors, such as newspaper style and differing times of delivery, Logan was able to make some tentative conclusions.

> ... the border zones of each state strongly prefer the paper produced in its own state ... On the other hand the boundary is not a rigid barrier. In Victoria, the *Advertiser* penetrates only in the municipalities adjacent to the border to any considerable extent. The Wimmera appears most attracted by the Adelaide publication probably because of the area's historical, economic and environmental association with the neighbouring South Australian regions and its location relative to the two metropolises.

In South Australia the whole south-eastern region is penetrated by the *Sun*. This may be seen as another effect of the region's isolation from its capital and its regional associations with Victoria.

(Logan, 1963, pp. 86–7)

When attention was turned to the local government boundaries of south-western Victoria, Logan found that they had little influence on the development of the cultural landscape. A motel and a drive-in cinema were located on the outskirts of Hamilton, in the Shire of Dundas, in order to take advantage of the shire's lower rates. This location was also close to the people who would use these concerns and offered access to the electricity and water services provided by Hamilton. Another case was discovered where different building regulations in two local government areas influenced landscape development. The less demanding building regulations of the Shire of Portland, which surrounds the town of Portland, allowed the growth of many holiday homes on the periphery of the town. The town authorities considered this development to be undesirable and in 1957 the shire also adopted the uniform building regulations.

Conclusion

The range of examples provided in this chapter indicates that geographers are aware of the influence which boundaries may exert upon the development of cultural landscapes. In most cases, however, the study has been only part of a work specially aimed at understanding the evolution of the boundary or the problems associated with it. It is to be hoped that in the future more geographers will give this aspect of boundary study closer attention, in order that a body of tested techniques can be formulated.

References

BLAINEY, G., 1949, 'The role of economic interests in Australian Federation: a reply to Professor Parker', *Historical Studies of Australia and New Zealand*, 13, pp. 224–37.
DAVEAU, S., 1959, *Les régions frontalières de la montagne Jurassienne*, Paris.

HOUSE, J. W., 1959, 'The Franco-Italian boundary in the Alpes-Maritimes', *Transactions*, Institute of British Geographers, 26, pp. 107–31.

KRISTOFF, L. A. D., 1959, 'The nature of frontiers and boundaries', *Annals*, Association of American Geographers, 49, pp. 269–82.

LOGAN, W. S., 1963, *The evolution and significance of selected intra-national boundaries in south-western Victoria*, unpublished dissertation for the degree of B.A., University of Melbourne.

MACKAY, J. R., 1958, 'The interactance hypothesis and boundaries in Canada: a preliminary study', *Canadian Geographer*, 11, pp. 1–8.

MINGHI, J. V., 1963, 'Boundary studies in political geography', *Annals*, Association of American Geographers, 53, pp. 407–28.

MINGHI, J. V., 1963a, 'Television preference and nationality in a boundary region', *Sociological Enquiry*, 33, pp. 165–79.

NELSON, H. J., 1952, 'The Vernon area of California – a study of the political factor in urban geography', *Annals*, Association of American Geographers, 42, pp. 177–91.

PARKER, R. S., 1949, 'Australian Federation: the influence of economic interests and political pressures', *Historical Studies of Australia and New Zealand*, 13, pp. 1–24.

PLATT, R. S., 1958, *A geographical study of the Dutch-German border*, assisted by Paula Bücking-Spitta, Münster Westfalen.

ROSE, A. J., 1955, 'The border zone between Queensland and New South Wales', *Australian Geographer*, 6, pp. 3–18.

SEVRIN, R., 1949, 'Les échanges de population à la frontière entre la France et la Tournaisis', *Annales de Géographie*, 58, pp. 237–44.

ULLMAN, E. L., 1939, 'The eastern Rhode Island–Massachusetts boundary zone', *Annals*, Association of American Geographers, 29, pp. 291–302.

5

Boundary disputes

Boundary disputes have long been a popular subject for research amongst political geographers. These subjects have a refreshing topicality, and generally result in the publication of much information useful to the geographer, which would not otherwise be available. The general term 'boundary dispute' includes four quite different types of dispute between political units having some measure of autonomy, for it must be recognized that disputes occur over the whole range of international and internal boundaries. This chapter will consider only international boundary disputes: internal boundary disputes will be examined in Chapter 6.

The first type of dispute may be described as a *territorial dispute*, and this results from some quality of the borderland which makes it attractive to the state initiating the dispute. The second type of dispute concerns the actual location of the boundary, and usually involves a controversy over interpreting the delimitation or description of the boundary. This type may be called *positional disputes*. Both territorial and positional disputes have as their aim a change in the position of the boundary, but the remaining two types do not require any change in boundary location. The third type arises over state functions applied at the boundary, and they may be described as *functional disputes*. The last type of boundary dispute concerns the use of some trans-boundary resource such as a river or mineral reserves. Disputes of this type usually have as their aim the creation of some organization which will regularize use of the particular resource, and they may be known as *disputes over resource development*.

Geographers are not alone in studying boundary disputes, which have also been a profitable field of research for political scientists, historians and international lawyers, but the facility of geographers with maps and their understanding of regional characteristics, have given them an advantage in such studies. There are clearly some aspects of boundary disputes which a geographer is not competent to consider, such as the involved decisions about the legality of treaties, and the role of individual persons in successfully pressing arguments in favour of one or another case. There still remains a great deal which the geographer can study in making a distinct contribution to understanding the situation. It is suggested that the analysis of any dispute should be aimed at discovering the initial *cause* of the dispute, the *trigger action* which creates a favourable situation for a claim to be made, and the underlying *aims* of the states concerned. The analysis should then continue to evaluate those *arguments* based in geography, and assess the *results* of the dispute, and its settlement if any, in respect of the borderland and the wider canvas of international relations.

This view may be illustrated by a brief consideration of one territorial dispute between Afghanistan and Pakistan. Afghanistan claims that the Pathan tribesmen in Pakistan should be allowed to form a state with their fellow tribesmen in Afghanistan; Pakistan in reply denies that the Pathans desire the establishment of Pushtunistan, as the proposed state is known. The basic *cause* of the situation can be found in the Anglo-Afghan Agreement of 1893, which delimited, by means of a map, the boundary between the spheres of influence of Britain and Afghanistan (Sykes, 1940, vol. 2, p. 353). This agreement was confirmed by further treaties in 1905, 1919, 1921 and 1930 (Hasan, 1962). This boundary divided the territory occupied by the Pathans in such a way that 2·4 millions remained within British territory. The *trigger action* which encouraged Afghanistan to make this claim was the partition of India in 1947, when Pakistan, facing internal difficulties and external pressure from India, replaced Britain as the sovereign neighbour of Afghanistan. The *arguments* advanced by Afghanistan fall into three categories. First it is argued that the 1893 treaty was not legally binding since Afghanistan signed it under duress; that in any case the tribal territories between Afghanistan and the administered territories of the British sphere formed independent territory, and that finally, Pakistan cannot inherit the rights of an 'extinguished person'; namely the British in India (Fraser-Tytler, 1953, p. 309). These are legal and moral arguments which the geographer can note, but not evaluate. Second, it is claimed that historically Afghanistan controlled much of India, and certainly the present area of western Pakistan (Taussig, 1961). Recourse to historical political geography shows that the State of Afghanistan was formed in 1747. At the maximum extent of the Durrani Empire in 1797, the area controlled reached eastwards almost to Delhi and Lahore. Lahore was ceded to the Mughal Empire in 1798, and Peshawar was lost in 1823. If territorial control for seventy-six years nearly one hundred and fifty years ago was accepted as a strong argument in favour of territorial reversion, the world map would be liable to dramatic change! Third, it is claimed that the Pathans in Afghanistan and Pakistan form a single ethnic unit, which should be united in one state. This argument is undoubtedly stronger, although Caroe (1961) has shown that the eastern Pathans have enjoyed close economic and political ties with the major states of the Indus valley, and have developed linguistic differences with the western Pathans. Further, the area claimed for Pushtunistan stretches from the Pamirs to the Arabian Sea, and is bounded on the west by Afghanistan and Iran and on the east by the Indus River. This includes large areas where there are few Pathans, such as Chitral, Gilgit, Baltistan and Baluchistan. When the strongest argument is exaggerated so remarkably as to weaken its force, one suspects the altruism of Afghanistan and seeks the real *aim* of this dispute. The claim to Baluchistan suggests that Afghanistan is hoping to control the proposed state and use it for an outlet to the Arabian Sea. Hasan (1962) has also suggested that the ruling Pathan dynasty in Afghanistan is seeking to bolster its position with regard to the Persian and Turki-speaking Afghans, who form two-thirds of the state's population.

The *results* of the dispute have been significant on the regional scale, and may become more important in the international scene. Diplomatic relations were broken between the two countries in September 1961 and resumed in May 1963. During this period the boundary was closed except for a short period in January 1962, when

American foreign aid supplies were allowed through from Pakistan. Since Afghanistan's major markets were in India and most of her supplies came from Japan, America and India, there has been some re-orientation of Afghanistan's trade. The Soviet Union now takes a much larger share of exports, and supplies more imports. Fighting in the area has also encouraged a programme designed to improve communications in the Pakistan border area. The closing of the boundary affected the traditional transhumance movements of the Powindas of Afghanistan. Normally about 100,000 Powindas with their vast herds migrated to Pakistan, as winter approached, from their summer pastures in Afghanistan. These people supplemented their incomes in Pakistan by manual labour, especially sugar-cane harvesting, and money-lending. Pakistan authorities required proper visas and other travel documents from the Powindas, who could not supply them. This move was apparently also made because winter grazing was scarce in Pakistan, and because the Powindas' herds carried disease (*The Times*, November 30th, 1961). Although the boundary has been re-opened, the movement of Powindas has now ceased and they are being re-settled under agricultural schemes which involve giving up their herds in Afghanistan.

On the international plane, it is noticeable that Afghanistan has been encouraged in its claim by India and the Soviet Union. It is understandable that the Indian Government will find comfort in the Pushtunistan diversion, since it reduced the pressure exerted by Pakistan against India in Kashmir. The U.S.S.R. presumably sees the dispute as an opportunity to weaken a member of S.E.A.T.O. and C.E.N.T.O., while at the same time strengthening her influence with Afghanistan, which had been a target for Russian diplomacy even in the pre-revolutionary period. Finally it can be noted that the situation becomes more complicated in view of the recent (1963) establishment of cordial relations between Pakistan and the People's Republic of China, at a time when Sino-Soviet relations are strained.

This brief account indicates the aspects of boundary disputes on which political geographers can most profitably concentrate. The remainder of this chapter examines the four types of disputes in detail, and concludes by examining the major boundary disputes in Africa.

Territorial disputes

While it is recognized that if a state feels sufficiently strong it may press territorial claims which have no basis in fact, nevertheless in most cases some arguments, however weak, may be legitimately raised. In such situations it will normally be found that the boundary does not accord with some meaningful division of the cultural or physical landscape. Since the boundary may be considered as a compromise between strategic, economic and ethnic requirements most boundaries will have some degree of unconformity, but in many cases it is not serious enough to encourage the development of a dispute. Clearly the boundary may have been superimposed, by colonial powers or by victorious states at the conclusion of a war, on an area which is already settled. The colonial boundaries of many states in Africa and Asia provide examples of the first situation. A simple example of the second circumstance is provided by the territory granted to Italy, south of the Brenner Pass, at the expense of Austria. This strategic boundary included many people of German or Austrian nationality within Italy and has been the subject of many claims by Austria. It is also possible for developments after the establishment of an antecedent boundary to create the conditions for territorial claims. After the states of Peru, Chile and Bolivia had been established, valuable guano and nitrate deposits were discovered in the coastal areas of all three states, especially in that of Bolivia. In Peru the deposits were developed under a government monopoly, while in northern Chile and southern Bolivia the smaller deposits of guano were developed by private firms, from whom the government derived duty when the material was exported. The manual work was done by Chilean peasants in this last case, and their presence in the Bolivian borderland, close to Chile, encouraged that country to make its successful territorial claims on the Bolivian littoral (Dennis, 1931, pp. 37 and 73).

Even if a boundary separates a state from a neighbouring area which has certain qualities of attraction, there is no certainty that a dispute will develop. Clearly a definite act is required by the claimant state to initiate the dispute. This action will usually be taken in the most favourable circumstances, and therefore it will often be noticed that a boundary which has created no problems for a very long time will suddenly become the subject of dispute. Generally the trigger action which creates the favourable situation is related to some change in government, or government policy, or the relative strength of the states concerned. The demands of the Philippines for North Borneo (now called Sabah) followed the adoption of a policy to create the Federation of Malaysia by uniting the territories of Malaya, Singapore, Sarawak, Brunei and North Borneo. Most observers feel that this claim was merely a device to delay and possibly frustrate the formation of Malaysia, which it was feared might yield to Communist subversion, threatening the Republic itself. The Sino-Indian conflict over Ladakh and the North-East Frontier Agency did not develop until China had achieved internal hegemony and re-established her authority in Tibet. Chinese foreign policy has been aimed at establishing what it regards as just limits with its neighbours, such as Mongolia, Burma and Pakistan; a policy which contrasts with her acceptance of boundaries established by the various colonial powers on the coast.

We can note that states rarely choose to negotiate from a position of weakness, and that sudden changes in state power results in the proliferation of territorial claims. After major wars there are always territorial disputes over enemy territory amongst the victors. The point is well illustrated by the case of Portugal at the Versailles Peace Conference. During the scramble for colonial territories in Africa the Portuguese-German boundary in East Africa was fixed through the mouth of the Rovuma River. In 1886 Germany claimed the Kionga triangle to the south of the river, and under duress Portugal ceded the area in 1894. After the defeat of Germany in 1918 Portugal successfully reclaimed the area at the Peace Conference.

In some cases it is an action by one state which induces the other to make a territorial claim. In 1915 and again in 1927 Guatemala made grants of land to the American Fruit Company in the area between the Matagua River and Meredon mountains. This immediately prompted Honduras to raise claims which had been dormant for a long period. In a similar fashion, the granting to the United States of a ninety-nine-year lease on the Great and Little Corn islands by Nicaragua encouraged Columbia to launch a claim that the islands were formerly part of the Province of Veragua and therefore belonged to Columbia under the principle of *uti possidetis*.

There are other developments which encourage states to press territorial claims. For example, many observers believe that Indonesia's claim to West Irian was forcibly pressed in 1962 in order to divert attention from the extremely difficult condition of her internal economy.

This poses the question of the aims of the state raising the territorial dispute. There appear to be two basic aims: the first is the strengthening of the state by the accretion of territory which possesses some attractive quality in respect of strategy or wealth; the second aim uses territorial claims as an instrument of policy. This last technique is a development which has recently been well illustrated in south-east Asia. The case of the claim by the Government of the Philippines to North Borneo and the Indonesian claim to West Irian have already been mentioned. There is also the case of China's territorial claims against India, which many attribute to the desire to force India to divert funds from economic projects to defence spending. It is rarely possible to gain definite confirmation of states' aims since such matters are often secret policy which can be determined only by reference to archives, long after the event. It is however useful to the research worker to understand the main aims of the contending states, as was shown in a recent study of the Anglo-French boundary negotiations in Kamerun after World War I (Prescott, 1963).

When the arguments in favour of any territorial claim are considered, it is useful to follow Hill's division (1945) which distinguishes legal arguments relating to a statement that the territory should belong to the claimant state, from other arguments which indicate that it would be more appropriate – or satisfactory – if the territory was ceded to the claimant state, but where there is no claim that the territory is illegally held. For example, the claim by the United Nations Organization against the Republic of South Africa for control of South-west Africa is based entirely on legal grounds. The United Nations claimed to be the legal successor to the League of Nations, but this interpretation was not accepted by the Republic, even though other mandatory powers placed their mandates at the disposal of the United Nations Organization. The Sino-Indian conflict in the North-East Frontier Agency is basically a legal conflict over the question of whether or not the Chinese Republic is bound by the Simla Convention of 1914 which defined the Macmahon Line. Geographers cannot make such a significant contribution to legal disputes as they can in the case of non-legal conflicts. The geographical significance of the application of treaties and conventions is a legitimate study of political geography, but no geographer would attempt to pronounce on the extent to which a treaty bound one or another signatory to its provisions. It is, however, useful for the geographer to understand the legal basis of claims to territory.

According to the General Act of the Congress of Berlin, legal rights to colonies in Africa could be secured only through effective occupation. Article 35 stated that the claimant state had satisfactorily to demonstrate to other states that the claim should be respected because a sufficient degree of authority was exercised throughout the area. This article was obeyed on the coast, but was honoured more in the breach than in the observance in the interior areas, where the states relied, often unsuccessfully, upon an unwritten hinterland doctrine. This hinterland concept is closely related to legal claims based upon contiguity or propinquity, although neither of these claims has foundation in international law. This point was made very clearly at The Hague Court when America tried to claim Palmas Island because of its proximity to the Philippines. Claims to parts of Antarctica based on the sector principle are well known, and have been used by states to support claims primarily based on prior discovery.

The legal basis of claims in South America is usually the principle of *uti possidetis*. This principle means that the new states accepted the same boundaries as the colonial territories they replaced. This was designed to ensure that European powers were prevented from making claims to some of the uncontrolled borderlands of the new territories. The principle is derived from the same term in Roman law, which applied to an edict which preserved the existing state of possession of an immovable object such as a house or vineyard pending litigation. The principle of *uti possidetis*, agreed by the new states in 1810, has probably worsened the territorial conflicts. There are at least two interpretations of the principle, and states tend to advance whichever suits them best. Some states regard the limits set as being those legally in force at the time independence was gained; while other states regard the limits as those which were observed for practical administration by the colonial authorities. For example, the Venezuelan Constitution in 1830 proclaimed the state as being coincident with the area previously known as the Captaincy-General of Venezuela. It was then discovered later that the Spanish administrators had in fact governed in good faith beyond their legal right. Venezuela then espoused the second interpretation in claims against neighbouring states.

Other claims to territory rest on conquest or cession. Britain's annexation of the Orange Free State and the Transvaal in 1900 was founded on conquest, and presumably India's present authority in Goa is similarly supported. Usually terms of cession are so clear that they are not the subject of dispute, even when the cession has been made under pressure, as was Portugal's cession of the Kionga triangle to Germany and Czechoslovakia's cession to the same state in 1938. When pressure of this sort has been exerted, the state which suffered often reclaims the land at a favourable opportunity, such as that presented by the termination of the first and second world wars.

The last legal claim considered is that of prescription, which means uninterrupted exercise of authority in an area, for a period which indicates that such actions are in accordance with international order. This is part of India's claim against Chinese counter-claims along their common boundary. It is not the only claim, but India maintains that Indian or British authority has been exercised in the disputed areas without Chinese objection (Rao, 1962).

The best current example of a legal claim is that to British North Borneo pressed by the Philippines. In 1877–8 a British syndicate secured the transfer to themselves of the rights of the Sultan of Sulu over the territories and adjacent islands, in return for the payment of a pension. According to the English translation the treaty stated that the land was ceded and granted forever and in perpetuity. In 1881 the syndicate was taken over by the British North Borneo Company, which received a royal charter in the same year. In 1883 the area was made a British protectorate, and in 1903 a confirmatory deed was signed by the Sultan specifying the islands which had not been individually named in the original treaty. In 1946 the area became a British Colony. The Philippine claim rests firstly on the ground that the Sultan was not empowered to sign the treaty since Spain was the sovereign power. This argument is not likely to produce results because Britain did not recognize the Spanish treaties with the Sultan in 1836, 1851 and 1864 since Spain could not control him. Furthermore, in 1885 Spain renounced her rights in favour of Britain, in return for recognition in the Sulu archipelago. America replaced Spain as the dominant power in the area in 1898, and Britain secured specific American recognition of her position in 1930. In case this argument proves unreliable, the Philippine Government relies on a second claim which interprets the treaty not as an unconditional cession of the territory but as a lease by the Sultan. This interpretation hinges on the translation of the Malayan word *padak*, which is rather milder than the translation 'granted and ceded'.

Only rarely does a claimant state rest its case on one line of argument. More frequently legal arguments are supported by non-legal points. These points usually refer to the historical, geographical, strategical, economic, and ethnic qualities of the territory which is claimed.

In most cases the historical arguments refer to periods that are not well defined and before the period when legal titles may have been gained. In 1919 France claimed the Saar on historical grounds, but its case was weak. Saarlouis alone had been founded by the French, under Louis XIV in 1680, but even this area had not been under French control for more than twenty-three years (Temperley, 1924, vol. 2, p. 177). Italy's claim to part of the Dalmatian coast at the same conference was based on strategic and historical arguments. The Italian Premier expressed the historical claim in the following sentences.

And can one describe as excessive the Italian aspiration for the Dalmatian coast, this boulevard of Italy throughout the centuries, which Roman genius and Venetian activity have made noble and great,

and whose Italianity, defying all manner of implacable persecution
throughout an entire century, today shares with the Italian nation the
same feelings of patriotism?   (Temperley, 1921, vol. 5, p. 404)

This type of statement seems typical of many historical claims which
often appear as padding to the more pertinent arguments.

Geographical arguments are normally designed either to show the
desirability of extending a state's territory to make the boundary
coincide with some physical feature, or to demonstrate the basic
unity of an area which is divided or is threatened with division. The
Banat was one such area at the end of the first world war. The
territory was contested by Rumania and Yugoslavia and is bounded
by the Danube, Tisza and Mureç Rivers. As in the Drava valley to
the west, the population is of mixed Magyar, Serbo-Croat and
Rumanian origin. The Yugoslavs claimed the lower central and
western parts, while Rumania claimed the entire area as a geographical unit. This view was based on the 'natural frontiers' which
the rivers provide and the complementary nature of the products
of the plains and the hills to the east, and the opportunity which the
plains afforded to the hill-dwellers for employment. The published
reports of the Sino-Indian boundary talks make it clear that India
rests much of her case on the 'natural boundary' provided by the
main watershed of the Himalayan system. It has often been noted
that a 'natural boundary' is one to which a state wishes to extend
and that there are no recorded cases of a state wishing to withdraw
to a 'natural boundary'. For this reason this argument is relied on
less than formerly and geographers must take some credit for
destroying the fallacy of the intrinsic merit of 'natural boundaries'.

The Greek and Yugoslav claims against Bulgaria at the Versailles
Peace Conference provide examples of strategic territorial claims.
In each case these claims were to territory at points from which the
German and allied forces had launched rapid and successful attacks,
and in that sense they were defensive claims. The Peace Conference
was careful to avoid reversing the situation by giving the claimant
states positions from which they in turn could launch a swift
penetrating attack. Russia's territorial claims at the end of World
War II seemed both defensive and offensive. The westward movement

of the Soviet boundary to the Bug River at the expense of Poland included the defensive Polesie marshes in Soviet territory, as well as the lakes of East Prussia which proved so useful to Germany during the last war. The cession of trans-Carpathian Ruthenia by Czechoslovakia to the U.S.S.R. gave this country a strong offensive position at the narrowest part of the Carpathians, overlooking the Hungarian plain. Control of the Tatar, Revetski and Uzhok Passes greatly facilitate any Russian invasion of Hungary. China's claim to the cis-Himalayan zone in Ladakh and northern Assam will, if realized, give it a strong defensive position in respect of the passes and a strong offensive position for any future southward advance.

The economic arguments in support of territorial claims are usually designed to show the economic integration with an area already held, the need of the area claimed as a routeway, or the value of the area as reparation for damage suffered during war. Czechoslovakia's claim to the Teschen district of Silesia rested on two main economic arguments. First, the Freistadt area was regarded as being inextricably linked with the industrial complex of Ostrava, where metal foundries depended upon the Karvina coking coal. The coal was also needed to a lesser extent in Bohemia and Moravia. Second, the Czechoslovakian Government claimed that the Olderberg-Jablunka-Sillein railway was of vital importance, since it formed the arterial line connecting Slovakia with Bohemia-Moravia. The railway through the Vlara pass, which Poland claimed could be further developed, was not considered suitable by the Czechs because of the steep gradients and sharp curves. Further, the only other line from Breclava to Bratislava was too far to the south. Poland reversed this economic argument to the east in Zips and Orava, when certain highland areas, occupied by people speaking a dialect transitional between Czechoslovakian and Polish, were claimed on the ground that they were more closely attached with Cracow, because of easy communication, than with Kralovany, the Czech county town.

Compensatory claims for property and population losses during the war were made against German colonies. Referring to Belgium's claim to Rwanda-Urundi, Temperley (1924, vol. 2, p. 243) notes that 'no one wanted to refuse the insistent claim of a state which had suffered so seriously from Germany's aggression in Europe'. The extension of Poland's territory to the Oder-Neisse line was also seen as compensation for losses through German action, as well as territorial losses to Russia, and the need to secure a better strategic boundary. Allied to such arguments are the cases where states secure territorial promises for co-operation with another state. A good example of this is provided by the 1915 Treaty of London between Italy and the Allied Powers, under which Italy agreed to merge her forces in the general war effort. Under this treaty certain territorial promises were made.

> In the event of the total or partial partition of Turkey Italy was to obtain a just share of the Mediterranean region adjacent to the province of Adalia.
>
> In the event of France and Great Britain increasing their colonial territories in Africa at the expense of Germany those Powers agree in principle that Italy may claim some equitable compensation, particularly as regards the settlement in her favour of the questions relative to the frontiers of the Italian colonies of Eritrea, Somaliland and Libya.
>
> (Temperley, 1924, vol. 4, p. 290)

Ethnic territorial claims may be based on many human qualities of nationality, race, language, culture and history. In the settlement of the boundaries of Poland and certain Balkan states at the conclusion of the first world war, strenuous efforts were made to draw boundaries which minimized the numbers of minorities. The intermingling of population in the European borderlands made it impossible to draw boundaries which precisely separated ethnic groups. In some regions such as the Western Banat, mentioned above, there was an intricate mixture of Yugoslavs, Rumanians, Magyars and Germans (Bowman, 1923, p. 272), whereas the Argyro-Castro area was claimed by Greece on the strength of the larger Greek rural population surrounding towns that were principally populated by Yugoslavs. The reverse situation occurred in the Klagenfurt Basin, where Yugoslavia claimed the entire area because of the dominant rural population, while Austria's claim was based on the Germanic population concentrated in the towns (Temperley, 1924, vol. 4, pp. 342 and 370). In some African territorial disputes based on ethnic grounds there has not been the same measure of tribal intermixing, and boundary adjustment could be made without transferring tribal minorities with the area (Prescott, 1959).

Disputes based on ethnic grounds have often been solved by plebiscites, especially when the solution was being imposed on the area, as in the southern section of the Klagenfurt Basin. In many cases, however, a plebiscite has not been found satisfactory because the state controlling the plebiscite area enjoys an important advantage in securing a favourable result. In 1883, the treaty of Ancon which terminated the Chilean-Peru war stipulated that the provinces of Tacna and Arica would be held by Chile for a period of ten years after which 'a plebiscite will decide by popular vote whether the territory of the above-mentioned provinces is to remain definitely under the dominion and sovereignty of Chile, or is to continue to constitute a part of Peru' (Dennis, 1931, p. 297). In fact no real attempt was made to hold a plebiscite until 1925, by which time Chile had sufficiently nationalized the area to make a favourable result certain. The plebiscite was never held and the commission appointed to conduct it noted that Chile's failure to provide the free voting conditions was the major obstacle.

It is now considered that there is little point in holding a plebiscite to settle the Kashmir dispute between India and Pakistan, since both states have taken those measures which seem necessary to ensure that the result would be favourable in the areas at present controlled.

Positional disputes

It is not proposed to deal in detail with such disputes, since a selection has already been considered in the chapter dealing with boundary evolution. The following paragraphs are designed to make some general points and to illustrate the common characteristics of such disputes. While the basic cause of territorial disputes is superimposition upon the cultural or physical landscape, positional disputes arise because of incomplete boundary evolution. It is not the quality of the borderland but rather the defect of the boundary which is crucial. Boundaries which generate positional disputes were often antecedent. This fact meant that once a line had been agreed there were often no good reasons to proceed quickly to its demarcation, which would have exposed the defects in the delimitation. The trigger action in the case of positional disputes is the development of previously little-used borderlands. The Red-river dispute between Oklahoma and Texas developed in 1919 when the Burkburnett oil-boom reached the southern bank of the river. Texas assumed that the southern bank lay within her jurisdiction, while Oklahoma insisted that the southern bank was the boundary. Confusion resulted when both States were making mining leases to cover the river bed. The final decision was that the southern bank was the boundary, but Oklahoma did not benefit to the extent expected since all beds of rivers which were unnavigable when the State was admitted to the Union belong to the Federal Government (Billington, 1952).

Similarly, France did not question the boundary delimitation between Northern Nigeria and Niger at the beginning of this century until it was discovered, by military patrols, that the *route practicable* linking Niamey and Zinder lay partially within British territory, to which the French were denied access.

Since area is not always a direct measurement of any territory's value there is little purpose in classifying positional disputes by the areas involved. It is, however, noteworthy that some positional disputes have involved very large areas. For example, the unsustained claim of Victoria to the south-east corner of New South Wales involved an area of 30,000 square miles (Ogier, 1902). There is probably greater justification for distinguishing disputes involving only a sector of the boundary from those where the whole boundary is in question; where, in effect, attempts are being made to nullify the delimitation. In this way the Anglo-German dispute over the interpretation of the shore of Lake Chad (Prescott, 1958) would fall into the sector group, while the classical dispute between Argentina and Chile, and the present dispute between India and China, are whole-boundary positional disputes. The first case has been thoroughly considered (Varela, 1899; Hinks, 1926; Ireland, 1938) and needs no further comment. The Sino-Indian dispute is of more immediate interest. (This dispute has been the subject of many indifferent studies. The best studies are by Kirk, 1960 and 1962, and by Rubin, 1960.) In this case both states are agreed that there is a well-marked boundary, but the locations claimed by both rarely coincide. This is not surprising when the treaties are consulted. In the western sector of the Sino-Indian borderland relevant Ladakhi-Tibetan treaties were concluded in 1684 and 1842, which referred to the boundary as follows:

1684 'The boundary fixed in the beginning, when Skyid-Ida-Ngee-magon gave a kingdom to each of his three sons, shall still be maintained.'   (Ministry of External Affairs, 1961, p. 51)

1842 'The territories of Ladahk as they used to be and the territories of Lasa as they used to be will be administered by them respectively without infringing upon each other.'
(Ministry of External Affairs, 1961, p. CR14)

While these agreements establish that a traditional and customary boundary exists they do not record its location. The historical evidence presented by India is challenged by China (Ministry of External Affairs, 1961, pp. 41–50 and CR53–70). Similarly, the Chinese historical evidence was strongly criticized by the Indian officials (Ministry of External Affairs, 1961, pp. CR33–52 and 56–70). The inability of the delegates to the joint talks to agree on any collection of common facts suggest that this boundary will have to be freshly negotiated. In passing we can note that the boundary dispute was initiated after Chinese forces had begun to occupy the border area and had constructed a road from Yencheng to Gartok, via the Aksai Chin region of eastern Kashmir. While the Sino-Indian dispute in the western sector is theoretically a positional dispute, it has many of the characteristics of a territorial dispute.

The arguments urged in positional disputes are generally legal and geographical. In the first case doubt will often be thrown on the legal meaning of an imprecise term, whereas geographical arguments will often indicate that the boundary definition does not accord with the terrain. Occasionally it will be argued, usually without success, that the final definition was contrary to the spirit of the agreement or treaty. The Anglo-German negotiations between Nigeria and Kamerun provide examples of the legal and geographic cases. The 1885 Agreement stated that the boundary from the coast to the Cross River Rapids followed the right bank of the Rio del Rey from its mouth to its source and then proceeded direct to the Rapids (Hertslet, 1909, p. 868). In 1888 it was discovered that the Rio del Rey was a channel eighteen miles long between two islands. There was no clear termination of the channel inland, because it merged into an intricate network of mangrove-fringed creeks, which gave connexion to two rivers. To the west was the River Akpayafe, to the east was the River Ndian. This discovery raised a vigorous controversy about which river should be considered as the continuation of the Rio del Rey. Neither government was disposed to make any concessions since the disputed territory might prove to be 'an Eldorado or a worthless swamp'.

In 1886 a further Anglo-German agreement established the termination of a second section of boundary as 'a point on the right bank of the River Benue, to the east of and as close as possible to Yola as may be found on examination to be practically suited for the demarcation of the boundary' (Hertslet, 1909, pp. 880–1). Britain argued, when the time came to select this point, that the term 'practically' had both political and economic meanings. Politically Britain would find it inexpedient to draw a boundary within sight of the walls of Yola, since the Emir of that important city was losing a considerable portion of his territory to Germany. Economically it was demanded that the boundary should be drawn to allow the free circulation of the people of Yola, which was later clarified to mean that sufficient area would be left to the east to provide satisfactory supplies of firewood and enough pasture. For Germany, of course, the term 'practically' had only a technical meaning in respect of the demarcation of the boundary.

An instance of a positional dispute arising because of allegations that the spirit of the agreement had been broken occurred in the Bornu section of the Anglo-French boundary dividing Kamerun in 1916. The British administration in Nigeria was advised of the boundary definition in a coded telegram:

> In German Bornu the boundary is roughly indicated by the curved line of Isaga, Uafisa, Gau, Kumbel and Kutelaka, thence in a north-western direction to Wulgo. (Prescott, 1963, p. 106)

It was found by the local officers that this line was superimposed upon the cultural landscape in that area, and in time they criticized it for this reason. The British Government in London could not understand the criticism until it was discovered that the telegram had been carelessly deciphered. The correct message read as follows:

> The following territories to be administered by us . . . Second, German Bornu. Boundary being indicated very roughly by a curved line . . .   (Prescott, 1963, p. 107)

By then the French had occupied as far as the line indicated and, although Britain stated that according to the Agreement *all* Bornu was to fall within the British sphere, France declined to relinquish the territory, which today forms part of the Cameroun Republic.

Functional disputes

It has proved difficult to find good examples of disputes which have arisen over the state functions applied at a boundary, other than in the case where an international boundary cuts across some primitive tribal group such as the Somali, or lies astride the transhumance route of pastoralists as in the case of the Powindas of Afghanistan. House (1959) has noted the effect of the 1947 boundary separating Italy and France in the Alpes Maritimes. As a result of the new boundary the French sector of one commune lacked sufficient summer pastures while the adjoining Italian settlement lacked sufficient spring and autumn pastures. Since positional changes in the boundary were not permissible a compromise, suggested by a Swiss arbitrator, allowed the Italian settlements certain grazing rights in France in exchange for certain rights over woodland in Italy. This assisted an earlier Convention, which allowed free circulation of persons and property within a zone twenty kilometres wide astride the boundary. This measure is similar to one recently concluded between Tunisia and Algeria, which allows the inhabitants of the borderlands of each state to cross the boundary without the formality of obtaining a visa. This has done much to facilitate the movement of workers from each side.

Disputes over resource development

The commonest source of such disputes are water bodies which

mark or cross any boundary, and the territorial waters and continental shelf areas. Disputes also arise over other trans-boundary
resources, such as minerals (Jones, 1945). It is proposed to deal
separately with the disputes associated with rivers and lakes and
with marginal seas.

Boundaries were often drawn to coincide with rivers in order to
allow easy recognition, and the disadvantages of such features as
boundaries have already been considered. In many other cases
however, except when the boundary coincided with a watershed,
river basins were divided between adjacent states. When the
boundary coincided with a watercourse the agreement usually contained a clause providing equal rights for nationals from both sides.
Generally the clause did not define the position with regard to the
tributaries of boundary waters, nor make provision for the joint
control of rivers which crossed the boundary. Often this was because
the border areas were under-developed and the use of rivers for
hydro-electricity and irrigation had not been envisaged. It is only
when the border areas became more closely settled and advances in
technology made possible the use of the rivers for purposes other
than navigation, that disputes about the use of boundary and other
waters developed. Many terms are used by different writers in
referring to rivers forming and crossing the boundary; it is proposed
here to distinguish three types. *Boundary waters* are those features
within which the boundary is drawn; this term is preferred to
contiguous waters used by Griffin (1959). *Tributaries of boundary
waters* form the second group. The term is entirely descriptive and
it is essential to distinguish the tributaries from the boundary waters.
Rivers which cross a boundary are called *successive rivers*. This is a
term suggested by Griffin which seems more satisfactory than any
other, such as 'divided rivers', since boundary waters are also
divided.

Griffin (1959) has shown that customary international law
requires that no action should be taken in respect of the boundary
waters which will diminish their value and usability to the other
state. The Guadalupe-Hidalgo Treaty of 1848 between America and
Mexico was explicit on this point, in respect of the Gila and Bravo
Rivers.

... neither (state) shall without the consent of the other construct any
work that may impede or interrupt, in whole or in part the exercise of
this right (free navigation): not even for the purpose of favouring new
methods of navigation.   (Miller, 1937, p. 217)

In fact an American company did interfere with the course of the
river and a Mexican complaint to the American federal courts was
successful, so that the Company had to make restitution to Mexico
(*American Journal of International Law*, 1912, pp. 478–85).

A dispute involving tributaries of boundary waters developed
between Britain and the United States in 1900. The Chicago municipal authority tapped Lake Michigan by means of a canal constructed
in the valley of the Chicago River. This resulted in sufficient water
to force the diluted sewage of the city through to the Des Plaines
River and thence to the Illinois and Mississippi Rivers. At that time
the canal was carrying 4,167 cubic feet per second away from the
lake. Residents of Missouri, through which the Illinois River flowed,
complained about Chicago's action, but it was found that the river,
as a result of the increased flow, was purer than before! Britain,
however, was concerned with the extent to which the lake levels
were being lowered, and by 1926, when the flow from the lake
through the canal was 8,500 cubic feet per second, it was estimated
that the levels of Lakes Michigan and Huron had dropped six inches
to a new mean lake level, while Lakes Ontario and Erie had been
lowered five inches. Since every inch represented sixty to eighty tons
carrying capacity in ships, it was demonstrated that the action of
Chicago was impairing the navigability of boundary waters. Britain
was successful in her action, and the amounts withdrawn from the
lake were diminished in 1927 to 6,500 cubic feet per second, in 1935
to 5,000 cubic feet per second, and in 1938 to 1,500 cubic feet per
second, which was within the amount allowed to American concerns
under the original agreement (Simsarian, 1938).

In considering the utilization of successive rivers it is clear that
the lower riparian may be harmed if the flow of water is diminished,
while the upper riparian rights may be infringed if the river is
dammed downstream to produce flooding beyond the boundary.
The classical example of the first situation concerns Egypt's anxiety

that the flow of the Nile should not be diminished through irrigation projects in the Sudan. This matter was carefully controlled through the Nile Waters Agreement of 1929, under which Britain undertook not to interfere with the quantity, level or date of the river's régime. The Sudan has continued to respect this Agreement, although there is not yet any agreement on how additional supplies of water should be apportioned. When Lake Kariba was formed on the Zambezi between Northern and Southern Rhodesia, Portugal demanded and secured guarantees of a certain minimum flow through Mozambique. This flow of 35,000 cubic feet per second is sufficient to allow navigation on the lower Zambezi throughout the year. At the same time the Rhodesian Governments gained assurances from the Union of South Africa and Angola that they would not draw additional supplies from the Zambezi above the lake.

Upstream flooding has often occurred. In 1897 the Canadian Dyking Company made a dam on Boundary Creek in British Columbia which resulted in the flooding of 80,000 acres of Idaho, which of course reduced the rateable value of that State (Simsarian, 1938). A contemporary example is provided by the Aswan High Dam in the United Arab Republic, which has flooded part of the Sudan and caused the resettlement of 35,000 Nubians in the Khashm el Girba area astride the Atbara River.

The Franco-Spanish dispute over the waters of Lake Lanoux provides a convenient example of how technological advances trigger disputes of this kind. Soon after the second world war France decided to dam the lake, which normally drained towards Spain, and force the water over a drop of 780 metres into the Ariège valley. The water would then be returned by a tunnel to the course of the River Font, which was tributary to the Serge River in Spain. A canal from the French side supplied water to Spanish irrigation schemes. Spain objected to this plan on the grounds that it infringed the Treaty of Bayonne of 1886. The eighth, eleventh and twelfth articles of the *Acte Additionnel* provided that both states had sovereignty over water within their boundaries; that the downstream riparian had a right to the 'natural waters which flow from higher levels without the hand of man having contributed thereto'; that the riparian rights of the upstream state should not be harmed, and that there should be consultation on all new works. Spain requested that France should make the dam less than the planned height to increase the natural flow towards Spain and reduce the electricity production by 10 per cent. France refused this request, and in 1957 the International Court adjudged that France's plan did not infringe the 1866 Agreement.

For the better maintenance of state security and the control of inshore fishing grounds, countries have normally claimed control over a strip of the surrounding waters. The width of this strip has varied, from a minimum distance of three miles, adopted by Britain, to twelve and more miles adopted lately by some countries. No figure has been internationally accepted as the legal limit of territorial waters. The state's sovereignty is absolute within territorial waters, although foreign vessels have the right of innocent passage. One of the most prominent recent disputes over the limits of territorial waters has been between Britain and Iceland, because an attempt has been made to prohibit British fleets from using certain fishing grounds.

Since World War II a second complicating claim has been made by many countries. These claims are to the continental shelf adjoining the state. This claim is quite distinct from the claim to sovereignty over territorial waters, since the state lays no claim to the waters above the continental shelf which lie outside the territorial limits. The first state to claim general rights over the continental shelf was the United States in 1945. The claim was made because of the need to explore under the sea for further deposits of petroleum and other minerals, which were often continuations of resources already being worked on the land. It was specifically stated that no interference with navigation would be involved. At the same time the United States reserved the right to declare certain conservation zones for high-sea fisheries. This decision largely resulted from the fact that Japanese salmon fishing fleets were intercepting Bristol Bay salmon making their run to the coast, and canning the fish in floating factories. This was ruining the American shore-based salmon fishing industry. The American claim was quickly followed by similar claims on behalf of many Central and South American states, and later Korea, states bordering the Persian Gulf, and Iceland and Australia.

The justification of these claims is sought in the rights which have been held by certain states over sedentary fishing grounds. For example, in 1881 the British administration in Ceylon claimed rights over the pearl fisheries in the Gulf of Manar, which are up to twenty-one miles from the coast. Similarly, in Queensland and Western Australia in 1888 and 1889 respectively, rights were proclaimed over pearl and bêche-de-mer fishing grounds. In a similar fashion France and Italy regulated the collection of coral in the Mediterranean waters off Algeria, Sicily and Sardinia.

The claims made by the various states differed widely. Peru, Chile and Ecuador claimed an area limited by a line drawn parallel to the coast at a distance of 200 miles. In 1954 five whaling vessels flying the Panamanian flag were arrested by Peruvian vessels at distances varying from 126 to 364 miles from the coast. As recently as 1951 it was held in two separate judgements that the doctrine of the continental shelf had not become part of the established rule of international law. These judgements were given in respect of disputes arising out of concessions entered into between the rulers of Qatar and Abu Dhabi, both Trucial Principalities, in 1935 and 1939 respectively. When the rulers proclaimed an extension of their authority over the subsoil lying beneath the high seas in the Persian Gulf, contiguous to their territorial waters, the oil companies claimed that they automatically received the rights to explore for oil in the extra-territorial waters (Lauterpacht, 1957, pp. 144–64).

In an effort to resolve the difficulties which would develop from different appreciations of the extent of the continental shelf, the United Nations held a conference on the law of the sea in 1958. The conference produced four conventions which related to territorial seas (although no provision was made for defining their width), the high seas, fishing and conservation areas, and the continental shelf. The conventions come into force after they have been ratified by twenty-two states. To date (October 1963) only the convention relating to the high seas has come into force.

The convention relating to the continental shelf defines it in the following terms.

. . . the seabed and subsoil of the submarine areas adjacent to the coast outside the area of the territorial sea, to a depth of 200 metres or beyond that limit, to where the depth of superjacent water admits of the exploitation of the natural resources of the said areas; to the seabed and subsoil of similar submarine areas adjacent to the coasts of islands.

(Department of External Affairs, Canberra, 1958, p. 370)

The first limit given follows the general definition of the continental shelf recorded in several dictionaries and geographical works (Stamp, 1961, p. 123). According to *The Times Atlas* (vol. 1, plate 1) the continental shelf is most extensive in a continuous area stretching northwards from the Cherbourg peninsula to Sakhalin. In the Pacific area other significant segments are found in the Sea of Okhotsk, the Yellow Sea, the western South China Sea and the Arafura Sea. The north and east coasts of North America and the Argentine and Antarctic coasts are the other principal areas where the continental shelf stretches over one hundred miles from the coast: the west coast of the American continents and the coasts of Africa have very narrow continental shelves. At the present time the exploitation of mineral resources on the continental shelf is not carried out at depths greater than 200 metres, but there is no reason why sedentary living organisms should not be harvested at greater depths than 200 metres.

The definition of the resources of the continental shelf is given in the second article of the Convention:

The natural resources referred to in these articles consists of the mineral and other non-living resources of the seabed and subsoil together with living organisms belonging to sedentary species, that is to say, organisms which, at the harvestable stage, either are immobile on or under the seabed or are unable to move except in constant physical contact with the seabed or subsoil.

(Department of External Affairs, Canberra, 1958, p. 370)

Young (1961) has shown that this definition lacks precision, and recommends a specific list of sedentary species. His argument is supported by the dispute between France and Brazil in 1962 over the question of whether lobsters remain in constant contact with the continental shelf. The French claim that they do not and can therefore be harvested by French vessels. The Brazilians claim that they do and therefore form part of the resources of the continental shelf and belong exclusively to Brazil.

The Convention makes quite clear that the rights conferred in respect of the continental shelf do not affect the status of the super-jacent waters as high seas or the air space above them. Further, the coastal state is required to avoid any interference with navigation, the laying of submarine cables and the carrying out of scientific research for open publication. Such features which have to be erected to allow exploitation of the continental shelf resources must not be located where they will interfere with recognized shipping lanes, and must be surrounded by a safety zone of 500 metres. This means that the states such as Chile and Peru who seek to use the continental shelf doctrine as a means of extending their territorial waters will not be able to make the Convention their tool. The last point of interest to geographers in the Convention are the rules laid down for dividing the continental shelf between adjacent and opposite coastal states. The line should be agreed between the states concerned, and if no agreement is possible then the median line equidistant from the base-lines from which territorial waters are measured should be used. To date only one case of dividing a conti-nental shelf between two opposite states has arisen. In 1953 Australia declared sovereignty over the surrounding continental shelf and declared a northern limit between Australian and Indonesian and Dutch territory lying midway between Australia and the other states. The same Proclamation also noted that there were certain areas contiguous to the continental shelf but separated by channels deeper than one hundred fathoms which were also claimed (Department of External Affairs, Canberra, 1953, p. 661).

Australia's unilateral declaration followed extensive fishing of pearl beds by Japanese fleets in the Arafura Sea. Australia main-tained that the amounts collected by Japanese vessels were in excess of the limits compatible with conservation of the resource. In the future, disputes over the limits of continental shelf rights are likely to occur between states fringing semi-enclosed seas such as the Persian Gulf, the Adriatic, and the Baltic Sea; and instances where hostile states such as Malaysia and Indonesia are separated by a continuous continental shelf.

Africa's major boundary disputes

The majority of Africa's international boundaries were delimited by European states during the two decades following the Berlin Congo Conference of 1884, and many of these boundaries were subsequently demarcated. The most important boundary changes since that period concerned the division of the former German colonies of Togoland, Kamerun and Tanganyika into British, French and Belgian Mandates after the first world war. Prior to European intervention there had been no boundaries in Africa. The indigenous political structures were separated by frontiers – disputed, often uninhabited zones – varying in width from two to twenty miles. Despite the popular criticism that the colonial boundaries were superimposed on the existing cultural landscape (Alexander, 1957, p. 325; Church, 1956, p. 748; and 1962, p. 533; Boggs, 1940, p. 156), research has shown that in many cases there was a genuine desire by the negotiating powers to preserve the integrity of recognizable indigenous states, such as the Sokoto-Gando Empire or the Kingdom of Buganda (Prescott, 1959 and 1961). However, the boundaries were not always drawn within the indigenous frontiers, either because the two European powers disagreed about the extent of the African states concerned, or because there were overriding economic or strategic interests.

The hardship occasioned to divided tribal groups was minimized by the inefficient way in which the boundaries functioned. The view that each colonial boundary 'represented the knife-edged divide between conflicting and contrasting colonial policies' (Church, 1956, p. 745) is misleading, first because many of the colonial authorities did not know the exact position of their boundaries, and second, because many of the officials, on each side of the line, avoided the exercise of authority to the absolute territorial limits, in order to obviate possible border disputes. Movement across most African boundaries was a simple matter for Africans, and the author discovered some Nigerian farmers, in the western region of Nigeria, who owned farms stretching into Dahomey, and who crossed the boundary at will.

The independent African states, which are replacing the colonial territories without any boundary adjustment, have not retained the same *laisser faire* policy towards their boundaries. Associated with this stricter control of the boundaries is the growth of pan-tribal movements amongst groups which had been divided by colonial boundaries, and which can now see political advantage and security in being united on one side of the boundary. Concern with territorial questions is a common characteristic of newly independent countries, and the new African states are not exceptions to this generalization. For example, the Ghana-Togoland boundary is carefully supervised by the Togolese Government, which fears political infiltration and the shipment of arms to opposition parties. In Nigeria, the Borgu section of the boundary with Dahomey is being demarcated in order to reduce tax-evasion, while the eastern border is being reinforced by a chain of police posts, aimed at preventing terrorists from Cameroun using Eastern Nigeria as a refuge. In the Horn of Africa, Ethiopia has arranged stricter control over her boundary with the Somali Republic, and has abrogated a treaty which gave Somali nomads the right to cross the boundary in search of pasture and water for their herds.

Africa's current boundary problems are evidence that some adjustment may be necessary if the colonial boundaries are to harmonize with the political attitudes and policies of the independent African states.

The Ewe problem of Ghana and Togoland

Latest figures show that there are 715,000 Ewe occupying the area between the lower Volta and Naho Rivers, which flow into the Gulf of Guinea. The northern margin of the tribe is found parallel to the coast and eighty-five miles inland. Most of this area consists of a gently sloping plain, rarely more than 1,000 feet in height, covered with an open savanna vegetation. The only variation is provided by the sandy beaches and palm-fringed lagoons of the coastal areas, and the bare, low granite inselbergs near the northern limit. With the exception of a few fishermen the majority of Ewe are farmers, cultivating yams and maize.

There have been persistent demands by some elements of the Ewe tribe for unification, either as a separate state, or as part of Ghana or the Togo Republic. The cultural uniformity of the Ewe is sufficient to justify their description as a tribe, but it will be shown that this measure of cultural homogeneity has not been paralleled by any political unity.

> It seems to have been left to the European administration to begin the welding together of the sub-tribes into larger centralized groups, and to the effects of European rule to create a national pan-Ewe consciousness. (Ward, 1949)

Before European intervention, the Ewe were politically divided into about 120 sub-tribes, lying between the centralized military kingdoms of Abomey and Ashanti. During periods of war temporary alliances were formed amongst the Ewe groups, but these were dissolved in times of peace. Eweland was first divided by the Anglo-German boundary which separated the British Gold Coast Colony from German Togoland. The boundary lay between Lome, on the coast, and the River Volta, thirty miles below Kpando. No complaint is recorded from the various Ewe groups at this time. After the first world war, the colony was partitioned so that France received two-thirds of the area, including the entire coastline and railways. The remaining area was contiguous with the northern Gold Coast Colony and was assigned to Britain. This boundary was confirmed in 1920, when Britain and France were granted 'B' class mandates over their respective sections. The opposition of some Ewe about Lome to this further partition of Eweland was unsuccessful, and at this stage the tribal area was divided amongst the Gold Coast Colony and the two Mandates. The effects of this threefold division were reduced because Britain administered her Mandate as an integral part of the Gold Coast Colony, unlike the French, who retained their Mandate administratively separate from Dahomey and Upper Volta. The Anglo-French division of the Ewe was felt acutely from 1941–3, when the Vichy Government closed the boundary. At the end of the second world war there were renewed demands by an invigorated pan-Ewe movement for Ewe unification, but there were conflicting suggestions about the mechanics of union.

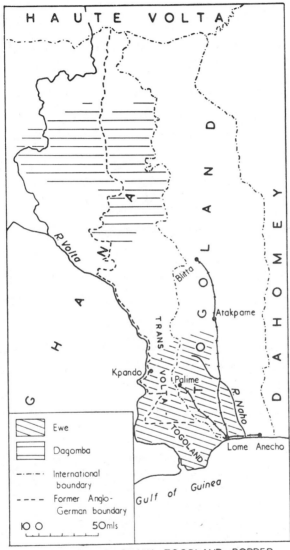

FIG. 3   THE GHANA -TOGOLAND BORDER

In 1950 a United Nations Commission made a report which contained the following statement.

> The problem has attained the force and dimensions of a nationalistic movement and a solution should be sought with urgency in the interests of peace and stability in that part of the world.
>
> (United Nations, 1950, p. 38)

No satisfactory solution to the Ewe problem has been found. In 1952 the Ewe area in British controlled territory was constituted into a Trans-Volta-Togoland region, which meant that the western section of the Ewe were administered as a single group. In 1956 a plebiscite was held in British Togoland, and a majority of voters favoured union with an independent Gold Coast Colony. Accordingly British Togoland was merged with an independent Ghana in 1957. In 1956, a plebiscite in French Togoland showed a majority in favour of the translation of the territory into an autonomous republic, within the French Union, but in 1960 the independent Republic of Togo was created outside the French Community.

It is difficult to imagine any other possibility which would have been more satisfactory. A re-unified Togoland would not have included the Ewe of south-east Ghana, and would have re-divided the Dagomba people of north-east Ghana. An independent Ewe state would not be viable and would have created serious problems of communication and development for the residual area of the Togo Republic. The Ewe of the Togo Republic regard union with Ghana as too high a price to pay for Ewe unification. The failure to satisfy Ewe demands has left a heritage of tension in the area. Relations between Ghana and the Togo Republic have deteriorated – periodically there are frequent charges and counter charges of intentions to invade – and the boundary is closely guarded on both sides. When President Olympio was assassinated in 1963 the Ghanaian boundary was immediately closed by the Togolese authorities. Ghana has repeatedly pointed to the advisability of a union between the two countries, and it is Ghanaian pressure, together with the strategic problems of defending the narrow Togolese territory from land assault, which has contributed to the unrest. Yet it is worth underlining that the Ewe have never known political unity. The original colonial boundary was not unrealistic; it is the changed political circumstances, and the rigid application of state functions at the boundary, which have created this problem.

Prescott (1959b) considered Nigeria's regional boundary problems, and although they still exist it is not intended to reconsider these problems here. There is some chance that the situation will become more tense since the new Mid-west Region was created in March 1964. The truncated Western Region may press its territorial claims against Northern Region and Lagos with greater energy.

The next major boundary problems to be considered are located in the Horn of Africa and the Colony and Protectorate of Kenya. The most important of the four problems concerns the Somali people.

The Somali problem

The Somali occupy the Horn of Africa, which is bounded by the Red Sea, the Gulf of Aden, the Indian Ocean, and an irregular line from the mouth of the River Tana in Kenya to the port of Djibouti in French Somaliland. The Somali are divided amongst French Somaliland (25,000), the Somali Republic (2,076,000), Ethiopia (350,000) and Kenya (119,000). There are two distinct Somali boundary problems concerned with the union of the Somali in Ethiopia and Kenya with those of the Somali Republic. There is no record of any agitation for the inclusion of the Somali living in French Somaliland.

Lewis (1955) refers to the Somali *nation*, but there is no history of political union under a central authority. However, while inter-tribal feuds are recorded, there is also a tradition of concerted action against the adherents of the Coptic religion in Ethiopia, and the Galla tribes of Ethiopia and Kenya. The community of language, culture and political organization is reinforced by an economy based on animal husbandry. Camels are the most important animals in the north and some parts of the south. Cattle are more important among the southern groups such as Digil and Hawiya, since camels succumb to diseases carried by the tabunus fly known as *baal*. Sheep and goats are herded throughout the area.

The only exceptions to a pattern of pastoralism with subsidiary cultivation are found in two regions between the Rivers Juba and Shebelle, inhabited by the southern Sab groups. These regions of the Bur Hakaba and Baidou plateaux possess black alluvial soils and a more reliable rainfall than the surrounding area. These twin advantages allow the intensive cultivation of sorghum, sesame, beans and cotton. It is only in these areas that there are fixed, known boundaries, marked by blazed trees. Elsewhere, effective occupation is the sole criterion of land control, with access to available pasture and watering points. The boundaries are in a state of dynamic equilibrium; the lands being used by one group shade into those of neighbouring groups and will change from year to year with variations in the strength and requirements of the various groups. In the more arid north of the Somali Republic, the pastoralists follow a nomadic pattern of life, tending to be in the upland pastures of the Haud, in Ethiopia, during the summer, when the Haud pastures are at their best and when the Somali plains are most uncomfortable. The southern part of the Somali area is distinguished not only by the greater amount of cultivated land mentioned earlier, but also by the transhumance movements of the stockherders. Herds and flocks are driven to the riverine areas during the dry season, for the Juba and Shebelle Rivers never become dry, and return to the interior pastures during the short wet seasons which last from April to May and from October to November. For some groups, such as the Marehan and Beidyahan, this movement involves crossing the international boundary between Ethiopia and the Somali Republic.

The colonial boundaries of Britain, France and Italy were superimposed upon the Horn of Africa during the period 1885–1900. Britain secured the East African Protectorate (Kenya) and British Somaliland, while Italy and France gained their Somaliland colonies. The initial geometric boundaries between Ethiopia (at that time Abyssinia) and the colonies divided tribal areas, often separating wet and dry season pastures (Clifford, 1936). During demarcation attempts were made to draw the boundaries coincident with territorial divisions between tribes. These attempts were bound to be unsuccessful since the tribes did not have fixed territorial boundaries. The fourth Article of the Italian-Abyssinian Convention of

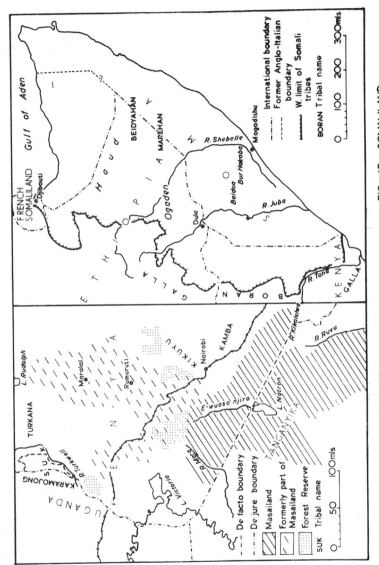

FIG 4A   MASAILAND

FIG. 4B   SOMALILAND

1908 stated that the boundary should be drawn north-east from Webi Shebali in such a way that

> . . . all the territory belonging to the tribes towards the coast will remain to Italy; all the territory of Ogaden and all that of the tribes towards Ogaden will remain to Abyssinia.   (*Trattati et seq.*, 1909, p. 177–8)

An Italian-Abyssinian Demarcation Commission began work in 1910 at Dule, but made little progress owing to the inability of the two sections to agree on the definition of tribal territory. Although the boundary between Ethiopia and British Somaliland was successfully demarcated in 1935, Somalis from the British colony had the right to cross the boundary to traditional pastures in the Haud – an arid plain sloping eastwards with little permanent water, except during summer, and covered by thorn bush – under the Anglo-Abyssinian Treaty of 1897.

Despite the colonial boundaries, continued Somali pressure against the Galla tribes in north-east Kenya displaced these people west of the River Tana. The number of Somali in Kenya was reduced in 1921 by the cession of the area between the River Juba and the present boundary to Italian Somaliland, in reward for participation in the first world war (King, 1928). To protect the Galla from further Somali invasions, a boundary known as the 'Somali line' was delimited sixty miles east of the River Tana, and the Somali were forbidden to move west of this line. This measure has not been successful, and the Somali groups are at present situated within ten miles of the east bank of the Tana River.

In 1935 there were disputes between Italy and Ethiopia, the most serious occurring at Ualual. In the same year Italy occupied Ethiopia, thus linking the Somalis of Ogaden and Italian Somaliland under one authority. In 1940 Italy also occupied British Somaliland, thus including the majority of Somalis under their control. Italian domination was replaced by Britain in the following year, and although Ethiopia regained her independence, Britain continued to administer the Haud and contiguous reserved areas. This meant that the Somali people were under British authority until 1950, when Italy was granted the United Nations Trusteeship of her former

Somaliland Colony. During the next ten years, before the Somali Republic became independent, Italy tried unsuccessfully to negotiate a boundary mutually acceptable to the Somali and Ethiopia. In 1954, Somali administrative unity was further reduced by the return of the Haud and reserved areas to Ethiopia, although a further treaty between Britain and Ethiopia guaranteed British Somalis access to their pastures in Ethiopia. The final stage in this area's political development has been the union of British and Italian Somaliland to form the independent Somali Republic. While this has given political unity to the Somalis of the former colonies, it has exacerbated relations with Ethiopia, who has renounced the Anglo-Ethiopian Agreement of 1954, concerning the rights of Somali from the Republic to use pastures in the Haud and reserved areas. Ethiopia claims that the Somali Government cannot inherit concessions granted to Britain; however no doubt is cast on the validity of the 1897 Agreement, which would not have been made without the concessions (Brown, 1961). This policy follows unsuccessful attempts by the Ethiopian Government to secure the loyalty of the Somalis within the Ethiopian boundary, and to attract the Republic to the idea of federation with Ethiopia, as has happened with Eritrea. Schools, hospitals and wells were promised in addition to the establishment of hydro-electric schemes on the Juba and Shebelle Rivers, but all Somali groups remain opposed to any compromise with Ethiopia, and it is an unfortunate fact that the Somali Republic is currently (1963) spending 20 per cent of its budget on military expenses.

While the Somali-Ethiopian dispute is of long standing, the claims of the Somali in Kenya for union with the Somali Republic have arisen since 1961. The two political parties amongst the Kenya Somali had agreed on their requirements for the future of their tribe. They demanded the secession of the Northern Frontier District, which is occupied in the east by Somalis and the west by the Boron, who bear many cultural similarities to the Somali, before Kenya became independent. They claim that the act of secession should be followed by a plebiscite, conducted by the non-African members of the United Nations Organization, when all Kenyan African troops and police have been removed from the territory. The nature of these demands, and the fact that they were made one month after Mr Kenyatta was released from captivity, indicate the real fear which these Hamitic Moslems have of the Bantu and Nilotic groups which led the demands for Kenya's independence. The Somali case for union with the Somali Republic is supported not only by a common culture, but also by the fact that the present geometric boundary divides tribal wet and dry season pastures, and by the remoteness of this area from the rest of Kenya. None of the conflicting Kenya political factions is prepared to consider the loss of two-fifths of the state's territory, which the arid Norther Frontier District represents.

Britain's final attempt to solve the problem involved creating the Somali area into a seventh Region of the Federation. This move was rebuffed, however, and the elections in 1963 were boycotted.

The other African boundary problems in this area were also associated with the approaching independence of Kenya.

The Masai problem

Masailand, which consists of 41,000 square miles of the eastern African Rift Valley, is occupied by 191,000 Masai. The area is divided between Kenya and Tanganyika by a straight boundary, so that 15,000 square miles occupied by 88,000 Masai lie in Kenya, while the remaining 26,000 square miles, peopled by 103,000 Masai, lie within Tanganyika. Most of the land is infertile and the low variable rainfall supports a parkland vegetation of thorn trees and medium to tall grasses. There are only two permanent rivers in Masailand – the River Ruvu marks the eastern boundary of Masailand in Tanganyika, and the E-wuaso njiro flows through the Kenya section to Lake Natron. The Masai are nomadic pastoralists: their cattle are kept near the permanent rivers during the dry season (June–November) and driven to the wet season pastures when they are available. Land rights are established by residence, and the limits of tribal pastures fluctuate from season to season.

Since neither the Tanganyikan nor Kenyan administrations have interfered with the movement of Masai groups across the boundary, except when outbreaks of rinderpest or pleuro-pneumonia occurred in the herds of one country, there should be no Masai boundary problem. However a problem is emerging, due to the new situation of a politically independent Kenya, and the mistrust with which the Masai regard the accession to power of the Kikuyu and Kamba agricultural tribes. These two northern neighbours of the Masai experience acute land-shortage, and the Masai fear that, in an independent Kenya, the Kikuyu and Kamba might overspill into the marginal farming areas of Masailand.

History shows that the Masai have cause for concern. Originally they occupied all the high plateau of Kenya, extending to Lake Rudolph. In 1889 rinderpest and smallpox epidemics reduced stock and population levels just at the time when European occupation was beginning. By 1904 land alienation had confined the Kenyan Masai to two Reserves – the first lying north of the Uganda railway between Rumuruti and Maralal, and the second lying between the railway and the Tanganyika boundary. In 1906 the northern Reserve was extended southwards, but five years later all the Masai in the northern Reserve were transferred to the southern Reserve, which was extended west to the River Mara and east to the Kikalelwa. The Reserve limits have remained unchanged since 1911, although 700 square miles were declared a Forest Reserve and therefore inaccessible to the Masai.

Although the Masai were aware of the political and educational advance of their neighbours and traditional enemies, they showed no desire to follow their example. On several occasions before Tanganyika became independent, Masai chiefs from both sides of the international boundary petitioned the British Colonial Office for Masai union and independence. This was not granted, and it is unlikely that the independent African governments will be more favourably inclined to the pan-Masai movement. The Masai in Kenya supported the federalist party, which once promised them access to sections of the White Highlands as they became available. It is significant that the Masai representative to the Kenya Constitutional Conference did not sign the document which created a quasi-federal Constitution for the territory. The Masai people have never known a greater measure of political unity than at the present time, even though the threat to their traditional way of life and tribal lands seems to operate only against the Kenyan section.

The two remaining boundary problems involving Kenya and Uganda and Kenya and Zanzibar arise from the fact that the convenient *de facto* boundary arrangements by Britain in respect of these colonies need to be established on a *de jure* basis, now that Kenya has become independent.

The Karasuk problem

The Karasuk area of Kenya, west of the River Turkwell, has been administered as part of Uganda since 1931 (Brasnett, 1958). This agreement was made because of the friction between the Suk groups of western Kenya, and the Karamojong of eastern Uganda. The Suk, subject to attacks from the powerful Turkana tribe in eastern Kenya, have in their turn maintained constant pressure against the Karamojong and occupied considerable areas of their dry weather grazing, south of Amudat. Tribal warfare reached a peak from 1920–30, and to reduce the level of fighting the border area between the two tribes was placed under the single authority of Uganda, by establishing a *de facto* international boundary along the Turkwell River in place of the *de jure* boundary which coincides with the western limit of the Turkwell catchment. Under the present arrangement the Uganda authorities have constituted the entire Suk area into Upe County governed from Amudat. This administrative unity has strengthened the political consciousness of the Suk, and has not prevented inter-tribal conflict. There is much unrest in this area, and the situation will be very difficult if an independent Kenya insists on restoring the *de jure* boundary, thereby redividing the Suk. Another area of unrest lies on the borders of Kenya and Ethiopia, where tribal raiding in 1962 cost the lives of 264 persons. Kenya and Ethiopia claimed in October 1963 to have resolved this problem.

The coastal districts of the Colony and Protectorate of Kenya

Since 1895 the mainland possessions of the Sultan of Zanzibar have been administered by Britain, as part of the East African Protectorate and its successor the Colony and Protectorate of Kenya, in return for an annuity. These possessions include a strip of territory ten miles wide along the coast, between the Tanganyikan boundary and Kipini, and the Islands of Lamu, Manda and Patta to the north. This coastal strip includes the valuable ports of Mombasa and Kilindi – Kenya's rail terminus and principal outlet. Originally the majority of the population of the coastal districts were Arab Moslems. They are now outnumbered by the Miji-Kenda Bantu tribes, which have always lived in the area, and members of the Luo tribe, which have entered the area to work in the main ports. The Arabs feared discrimination by an independent African government, and called for reunion of the coastal districts with Zanzibar. Clearly before Kenya became independent the position needed clarification.

Sir James Robertson, commissioned to report on the situation by the British Government, recommended that the area should be included within Kenya (*The Times*. December 20th, 1961, pp. 9 & 11). Such a step was recommended on the grounds that it was demanded by the African majority of the territory; that Balkanization of African territories should be discouraged; and that Kenya should retain control of the vital ports. In order to safeguard the rights of the Moslem minority, it was further recommended that the coastal territory should be one of the regional units in an independent Kenya, and should be made the capital territory in the event of a Federal constitution being established. The problem was solved along these suggested lines in 1962, although Nairobi is the country's Federal capital.

Two other disputes remain to be considered at opposite ends of the continent. In the north-west, Morocco lays claim to the northern Spanish colonies and Mauretania, and a portion of Algeria near Tindouf. The claims against the first two areas are based in history, and while Moroccan authorities do not seem to be pressing their claims to the point of open conflict, their representatives boycott international meetings at which Mauretania is represented in case this is interpreted as recognition of this government. The claim against Algeria results from the fact that the boundary between these former French areas was never delimited, although it was fairly effectively demarcated by mine-fields laid by the French forces during the Algerian war of independence. The area claimed by

Morocco includes high-grade iron ore reserves totalling 650 million tons. Algeria resists the claim and retains the former French mine-fields!

In southern Africa there is the legal dispute between the Republic of South Africa and certain members of the United Nations, who claim that South Africa's responsibilities under the mandate of South-West Africa, granted by the League of Nations, are now due to the United Nations, which is the League's legal successor. This view is rejected by South Africa and it seems that even adverse advisory opinions by the International Court of Justice will not persuade South Africa to change her attitude. This is entirely a legal dispute to which the geographer cannot contribute, although it is worthwhile noting that the dispute is being prosecuted more vigorously by certain states as the colonial areas of the world diminish and as the recently independent states become more nfluential in world forums.

Conclusion

All the African disputes discussed above are territorial in character, and with the exception of the cases of South-West Africa and Morocco, they are based on ethnic causes. These ethnic disputes, together with the problems related to the Ijaw, Ibo and Yoruba groups in Nigeria, have three common features. First, they are all concerned with divided tribal groups. Second, all the disputes concern present or former British colonies, or occupied areas. This suggests that the British policy of indirect rule through the indigenous politico-tribal structure has maintained a high level of tribal consciousness, and this view is supported by the absence of problems in former French colonies, where official policies have resulted in a considerable measure of detribalization. Third, although the histories of some of the problems can be traced to the first decade of this century, they have all become more acute in the post-1945 period of African nationalism and the transfer from colonial to autonomous government. This development seems to result partly from the increased concern of independent African states with their boundaries, and partly from the fear by minority groups of discrimination by the larger tribes, who were often traditional enemies.

Short of changing the position of the disputed boundaries, it seems that these ethnic boundary problems will be eased by the state functions applied at the boundaries being maintained at a low level, as in the Sahel-Benin Entente, and by the provision of constitutional safeguards for minority groups. It must be noted that the attempts to create quasi-federal organizations out of the unitary states of Kenya or the former Belgian Congo may increase the number of ethnic boundary problems.

None of the boundary problems relate to the unsatisfactory nature of boundary delimitation or demarcation, although few tropical African boundaries are satisfactory in these respects. Such disputes may arise when border areas are more intensively developed, or if there is an attempt to utilize trans-boundary resources such as rivers or mineral resources.

References

ALEXANDER, L. M., 1957, *World political patterns*, Chicago.

BILLINGTON, M., 1959, 'The Red River boundary controversy', *Southwestern Historical Quarterly*, 62, pp. 356–63.

BOGGS, S. W., 1940, *International boundaries*, New York.

BOWMAN, I., 1923, *The new world*, London.

BRASNETT, J., 1958, 'The Karasuk problem', *Uganda Journal*, 22, pp. 113–22.

BROWN, D. J. L., 1961, 'Recent developments in the Ethiopia-Somaliland frontier dispute', *International and Comparative Law Quarterly*, 10, pp. 167–78.

CAROE, SIR O., 1961, 'Pathans at the crossroads', *Eastern World*, 15, 12, pp. 12–13.

CHURCH, R. J. H., 1962, *West Africa*, London.

CHURCH, R. J. H., 1956, Chapter 21, 'African boundaries', in East, W. G., and Moodie, A. E., (Eds.), 1956, *The changing world*, London.

CLIFFORD, E. H. M., 1936, 'The British-Somaliland-Ethiopia boundary', *Geogr. J.*, 87, pp. 289–307.

DENNIS, W. J., 1931, *Tacna and Arica*, New Haven.

DEPARTMENT OF EXTERNAL AFFAIRS, CANBERRA, 1958, *Current notes on international affairs*, Canberra.

FRASER-TYTLER, SIR W. K., 1953, *Afghanistan*, London.

GRIFFIN, W. L., 1959, 'The use of international drainage basins under customary international law', *American Journal of International Law*, 53, pp. 50–80.

HASAN, K., 1962, 'Pakistan-Afghanistan relations', *Asian Survey*, 11, pp. 14–19.

HILL, N. L., 1945, *Claims to territory in international law and relations*, London.

HERTSLET, SIR E., 1909, *Map of Africa by Treaty*, London.

HINKS, A. R., 1921, 'Notes on the techniques of boundary delimitation', *Geogr. J.*, 58, pp. 417–43.

HOUSE, J. W., 1959, 'The Franco-Italian boundary in the Alpes-Maritimes', *Transactions*, Institute of British Geographers, 26, pp. 107–31.

IRELAND, G., 1938, *Boundaries, possessions and conflicts in South America*, Cambridge, Mass.

JONES, S. B., 1945, *Boundary making: a handbook for statesmen*, Washington.

KING, L. N., 1928, 'The work of the Jubuland Boundary Commission, *Geogr. J.*, 72, pp. 420–34.

KIRK, W., 1960, 'The Sino-Indian frontier dispute', *Scottish Geographical Magazine*, 76, pp. 3–13.

KIRK, W., 1962, 'The inner Asian frontier of India', *Transactions*, Institute of British Geographers, 31, pp. 131–68.

LAUTERPACHT, SIR H., 1957, *International Law Reports*, 1951, London.

LEWIS, I. M., 1955, *Peoples of the Horn of Africa*, London.

MILLER, H., 1937, *Treaties and other international acts of the United States of America*, 5, Washington.

MINISTRY OF EXTERNAL AFFAIRS, 1961, *Report of the officials of the Governments of India and the People's Republic of China on the boundary question*, New Delhi.

OGIER, J. C. H., 1902, 'The question of the original official boundary between the states of New South Wales and Victoria', *Victorian Geographical Journal*, 20 (New series), pp. 71–84.

PRESCOTT, J. R. V., 1959a, 'The evolution of Nigeria's boundaries', *Nigerian Geographical Journal*, 2, pp. 80–104.

PRESCOTT, J. R. V., 1959b, 'Nigeria's regional boundary problems', *Geogr. Rev.*, 49, pp. 485–504.

PRESCOTT, J. R. V., 1961, 'La géographie politique du Cameroun Septentrional sous mandat britannique', *Annales de Géographie*, 377, pp. 86–90.

PRESCOTT, J. R. V., 1963, 'The evolution of the Anglo-French inter-Cameroons boundary', *Nigerian Geographical Journal*, 5, pp. 103–20.

RAO, K. K., 1962, 'The Sino-Indian border question and international law', *International and Comparative Law Quarterly*, 11, pp. 375–415.

RUBIN, A. P., 1960, 'The Sino-Indian border dispute', *International and Comparative Law Quarterly*, 9, pp. 96–125.

SIMSARIAN, J., 1938, 'The division of waters affecting the United States and Canada', *American Journal of International Law*, pp. 488–518.

STAMP, L. D. (Ed.), 1961, *A glossary of geographical terms*, London.

SYKES, SIR P. M., 1940, *History of Afghanistan*, 2 vols., London.

TAUSSIG, H. C., 'Afghanistan's big step', *Eastern World*, October, p. 15.

TEMPERLEY, H. W. V., 1920–24, *History of the Peace Conference of Paris*, 4 vols., London.

TRATTATI, CONVENZIONI, ACCORDI, 1909, *Protocolli et altri Documenti Relativi all Africa 1884–1908, Supplemento all Raccolta*, Rome.

UNITED NATIONS, 1950, *Special report of the first visiting Mission to the Trust Territories of Togoland under British administration and Togoland under French administration on the Ewe problem.*

VARELA, L. V., 1899, *Le république Argentine et le Chili: Histoire de la démarcation de leurs frontières*, 2 vols, Buenos Aires.

WARD, B. E., 1949, *The social organization of the Ewe-speaking people*, M.A. thesis, University of London.

YOUNG, R., 1961, 'Sedentary fisheries and the convention on the continental shelf', *American Journal of International Law*, 55, pp. 359–73.

6

Geographical studies of intra-national boundaries

An examination of the numerous boundary studies by geographers, historians and lawyers reveals that the majority are concerned with international boundaries and the minority with intra-national boundaries. It is the aim of this chapter to review intra-national boundary studies, in order to determine their subjects and methodology, and to show their relation with the better known international boundary studies. There are two main types of intra-national boundaries – federal and internal. Federal boundaries separate states within a federation, while internal boundaries mark the limits of administrative units within the individual federal states or unitary states. If this classification is accepted it means that there is a threefold hierarchy of boundaries – international, federal and internal. (A fourth category – extra-national – could refer to the boundaries of international organizations, such as the North Atlantic Treaty Organization, but they would usually be sections of existing international boundaries.) A federal state would possess all three categories, while a unitary state would possess only international and internal boundaries. Clearly all these categories can then be further subdivided according to the well-known sequential functional and morphological classifications.

The characteristics of international, federal and internal boundaries

Before reviewing intra-national boundary studies it seems worthwhile to examine the characteristics of the three groups of boundaries. International and federal boundaries are normally delimited through bilateral or multilateral negotiation, whereas internal boundaries are based on unilateral decisions of a single sovereign power. This means that international and federal boundaries are less susceptible to change than internal boundaries, which can be varied according to the needs of the state. International and federal boundaries have many functions, while there may be different patterns of internal boundaries to serve separate functions. The combination of these two differences generally results in the international and federal boundaries being more deeply intrenched into the landscape than internal boundaries. Internal boundaries are often not demarcated in contrast with the other two categories, where provision is generally made for demarcation, although it may not always be carried out.

The often ephemeral nature of internal boundaries makes it much more difficult to trace their evolution in function and position than that of international and federal boundaries, which are usually defined in some published treaty. Internal boundary changes are usually published in a Government gazette, and can be very difficult to follow. Freedom of movement across federal and internal boundaries makes it easier to carry out fieldwork in respect of these two categories than is the case with most international boundaries. Lastly it seems likely that people are more aware of the influence on their lives of federal and internal boundaries than of international boundaries. This is because federal and internal boundaries may determine the level of taxation, the requirements to be observed in building a home, the state schools available for children, and the quality and quantity of cultural amenities such as libraries.

The following sections consider those aspects of intra-national boundaries appropriate for geographical study and the methods which may be used.

The evolution of federal and internal boundaries

Geographers are concerned with the evolution of boundaries in respect of definition, function and position, and it is important to realize that evolution in these respects may be related or take place separately. For example, in 1917 the latitudinal boundary which had *allocated* territory between the Northern and Southern Provinces of the Colony and Protectorate of Lagos was *delimited*. This change in definition was accompanied by a change in position which transferred 5,650 square miles to the Northern Provinces, but the function of the boundary remained unchanged. On the other hand, in 1921 the international boundary between Eire and Northern Ireland was created from existing county boundaries without any changes in definition or position.

Studies are available dealing with the evolution of the federal boundaries of the United States, Canada, Australia, the Soviet Union and Nigeria. The development of Nigeria's federal boundaries is distinct from the other four cases: first, because the area which became Nigeria had a large settled indigenous population long before the boundaries were drawn by colonial administrators; second, because the boundaries reached their present form as the primary internal boundaries of a unitary state – the Colony and Protectorate of Nigeria; and third, because there was no attempt to colonize the area by large numbers of Europeans. In Australia and North America the boundaries were drawn in areas being colonized by Europeans, who were opposed by numerically small indigenous groups, lacking political hegemony. Nor did any of these federal states experience a period of unitary government involving the whole of their present territory.

Taking the example of Nigeria first, we find that the existing three federal states and their boundaries can be traced to the original threefold division of the Nigerian coast amongst the Lagos Colony and Protectorate, the Royal Niger Company Treaty Area and the Niger Coast Protectorate from 1892–8. None of these boundaries was demarcated. The boundaries of the Lagos Colony and Protectorate were intended to coincide with the known limits of the Yoruba Confederation based on Ijebu, Abeokuta and Ibadan, which were clearly distinguished from the hostile Yoruba groups around Ilorin, and the Edo Kingdom of Benin to the east. The other boundaries between the Niger Coast Protectorate and the R.N.C. Treaty Area were arbitrary and resulted in the division of the Niger Coast Protectorate into two sections east and west of the River Niger and its delta. In 1900 the charter of the Royal Niger Company was revoked, and three British Protectorates occupied the area of Nigeria. The Niger Coast Protectorate became the Protectorate of Southern Nigeria and was expanded to include the former Royal Niger Company Treaty Area south of the latitude of Idah – seven degrees ten minutes North.

In 1906 the two southern Protectorates were united, and in 1914 they amalgamated with the Northern Protectorate to create a unitary state with its capital at Lagos. The primary division into Northern and Southern Provinces was retained.

> In 1917 the boundaries of the Northern and Southern Provinces – drawn when the territory had not yet been explored and depending upon no geographical or ethnological features – were carefully revised so as no longer to bisect tribal units, except where by the usage of seventeen years a fraction of a tribe had become incorporated with its neighbours.   (Report on Amalgamation *et seq.*, 1920, p. 11)

In 1939, the present boundary between the Eastern and Western Regions was created from existing provincial boundaries. It reflected the distinction between the mature political organization of the Benin and Yoruba groups west of the Niger, and the organization of the Sobo, Ibo and Ibibio groups east of the river, which had not advanced beyond the clan or family level. These three Regions formed the Federation of Nigeria in 1954, and although the boundaries acquired fresh functions in respect of taxation, education and land ownership, there was no change in position or definition. The federal boundaries have not been satisfactorily demarcated and are difficult to trace except near main roads and along the railways.

In the United States and Canada, the different federal boundary evolution between the eastern region and the remainder of the continent has been recognized by Nicholson (1954), Deutsch (1960) and Whittlesey (1956). In the eastern margin of the continent the first boundaries, which allocated territory, were antecedent to settlement, but modification to the final boundary form was subsequent to the expansion of farmlands and settlements from separate coastal locations. These eastern colonies formed the nuclei of the present States. New States were added by the division of western areas as the nuclei of mining (British Columbia) and agricultural activity (Manitoba) became established. Although Brice, writing of the western States of the United States of America, claims that the federal boundaries are entirely arbitrary, Deutsch, Ullman and Whittlesey have shown that the boundaries represent the compromise between opposed local political forces, often based on sectional economic interests, and the desire to admit slave and free territories in pairs between 1800–50. Further, once a State was admitted, its boundaries became inviolate, even if the subsequent appreciation of the environment and of settlement trends indicated the need for adjustment. Apart from the creation of Washington D.C., only two States have yielded territory to new jurisdictions: part of Massachusetts was transferred to Maine, and Virginia was divided to create the two States of Virginia and West Virginia. In Canada also, the State areas could not be diminished once they had been established, and Nicholson has shown that the underlying principle was the desire to create States or Provinces with approximately equal areas. This situation was revealed by the extensions of Alberta and Saskatchewan in 1905 and the additions to Manitoba, Ontario and Quebec in 1912 (Nicholson, 1954, p. 119).

The federal boundaries of Australia evolved between 1826 and 1862 as the boundaries of separate British colonies. With the exception of the Tasmanian limits, the State boundaries were arbitrarily drawn to enclose coastal concentrations of settlement at Perth, Sydney, Brisbane, Melbourne and Adelaide. When the Australian Commonwealth was formed, the change in boundary functions was not accompanied by any change in boundary position or definition.

Shabad (1956) and Morrison (1938), in studying the intra-national boundaries of the Soviet Union, have shown that both federal and internal boundaries have been frequently altered to conform with significant changes in population distribution and industrial development. The Soviet boundaries show a higher correlation with the geographical divisions of the cultural landscape than the equivalent boundaries in America and Australia.

Of the writers considered, only Nicholson and Prescott have treated the evolution of federal boundaries in respect of definition, recognizing the stages of allocation, delimitation and demarcation, proposed by Jones (1945). Apart from these studies, and papers by Thomas (1949) on the demarcation of the federal boundaries of

Idaho, and Griswold (1939) on the demarcation of federal boundaries in the north-east United States, there is a lack of studies related to boundary definition which contrasts with the multitude of studies concerned with the definition of international boundaries in Africa, Asia and South America.

All the papers dealing with boundary evolution adopt an historical approach, and while this is logical and clear, it is regrettable that none of the writers has used two useful methods suggested by Hartshorne (1950) and Day (1949). In considering the Franco-German boundary of 1871 Hartshorne considered the relative importance of three factors – nationality, strategy and the distribution of iron ore resources – in determining the final position of the boundary. It is clearly demonstrated that different factors were paramount in determining different parts of the line, and that the distribution of iron ore reserves played a minor role. Although Hartshorne was concerned with one set of boundary negotiations which occupied only a short period, the author has satisfied himself that this technique could be used to show how the factors influencing the evolution of the Anglo-French colonial boundaries in Africa changed over a much longer period, involving several sets of negotiations.

Writing on the boundaries of India during the Hindu and Mughul Empires, Day indicated the value of considering boundary permanence, and this technique was used by Spate (1957), who greatly improved the cartographic representation of boundary permanence. Day showed the various boundaries over a period of time as separate lines, and in fact displaced coincident boundaries to avoid confusion. Spate represented the various boundaries by lines which had a thickness proportional to their permanence. This has produced a very striking and stimulating map. There is, however, still room for improvement in this method. It would be valuable if those boundaries still in use could be distinguished on a map so as to reveal any anomalies. In addition it would be valuable to discover some way of distinguishing between various periods when the boundary served different functions. For example, it would be unsatisfactory to show a boundary which had existed for eighty years as an internal boundary and twenty years as an international boundary by the same symbol as represented an international boundary which had existed for one hundred years. It is to be hoped that future studies of federal boundary evolution will make use of these neglected methods.

Only two articles dealing with the evolution of internal boundaries have been discovered. Fenelon (1956) deals with the geographical structure and boundaries of the Departments of France, and considers in broad outline the relationship between the modern boundaries and the former diocesan and county limits. He also refers to the relation between political boundaries and physical features. Yonekura (1956) traces the evolution of the forty-six *ken* of modern Japan. They bear a close relationship to the sixty-eight *kuni* of the seventh century, which were administrative divisions with populations varying from 50,000–100,000 and which were bounded by physical features such as rivers or watersheds. The *kuni* boundaries survived the establishment of feudal provinces which existed from the eighth to the mid-eighteenth centuries, within boundaries which were superimposed upon the *kuni* pattern. Yonekura's general conclusion, that the political-administrative divisions of a country may form a 'regional provincial system' or a 'departmental system', having their origins in the feudal middle ages and ancient civilizations respectively, needs further substantiating by examples from states other than Japan. It is further recommended that the use of adjectives such as 'provincial' and 'departmental' should be avoided in coining general terms, since they have widely different meanings in different countries.

Two reasons may account for this apparent neglect of studies of the evolution of internal boundaries. First, internal boundaries are often subject to rapid change, and second, the notification of internal boundary changes are often difficult to locate. In making a study of the evolution of Nigeria's provincial boundaries it was necessary to collect material from a wide variety of sources in the National Archives at Ibadan, and from provincial headquarters throughout the Federation. In view of the lack of other studies it seems worthwhile to outline briefly the evolution of Northern Nigeria's provincial boundaries.

Two stages can be recognized in the evolution of the Provinces and their boundaries in Northern Nigeria. The stages are multiplication and integration. The stage of multiplication was concerned with the pacification of the territory. Boundaries were traced in bold lines on sketch-maps and indicated the limits of military jurisdiction, within which the indigenous population was contacted and pacified if necessary. As the area over which the Government exerted direct authority was increased, new Provinces were created. Once the Government had succeeded in establishing effective control over the whole territory the second stage commenced. Colonial administrations were encouraged to be thrifty, and one way of reducing expenditure was to have an efficient administrative system with the fewest possible Provinces and provincial offices. Accordingly some of the earlier Provinces were amalgamated, and the boundaries were drawn with a view to assisting administrative efficiency and economy. By empirical methods a structure of Provinces was evolved. At first there were large-scale changes, but these gradually became smaller and fewer in number as a satisfactory condition was achieved. When this stage was reached closer delimitation of the boundaries was undertaken, and in some cases residents organized a simple kind of demarcation, mainly for their own references and to avoid inter-provincial disputes.

When the Protectorate of Northern Nigeria was created in 1900, the Government of that territory immediately organized the territory over which the Royal Niger Company (R.N.C.) had exerted control, into nine Provinces – Borgu, Ilorin, Kabba, Nupe, Upper and Lower Benue, Kontagora, Zaria and the Middle Niger. The first aims of the new administration were to organize Bassa, which lay south of the Benue, and the Muri, Bautshi and Yola Emirates. The reasons given for this eastward advance were threefold. First, it was necessary to prevent any further depopulation of this area by slave raids; second, it seemed worthwhile to open up the trade routes in that area and counter French activities south of Lake Chad; and third, it was decided to exploit the reported 'salubrity and mineral wealth' of the area.

In 1901 the Middle Niger Province was absorbed by Kabba Province and five new Provinces were created – Bassa, Bautshi, Yola, and North and South Bornu. This brought the total number of

Provinces to thirteen and it was increased to sixteen in the following year by the addition of Sokoto, Kano and Katagum. This meant that apart from Gando the entire area had been nominally placed under control. There were two reasons for this rapid northward drive. First, the government of the Protectorate could not feel secure while the strongest Fulani Emirates remained outside their control. Further, the continued independence of the northern Emirates created dual loyalties for the southern rulers, such as the Emirs of Bida and Kontagora, who had accepted British rule, and impaired their spirit of co-operation. Second, there was the need to occupy the Sokoto arc across which French columns were travelling between Niamey and Zinder. This occupation was designed to repair British prestige and to make the French position at Zinder untenable by denying access to the *route practicable*. The year 1904 marked the end of the period of multiplication when Gando Province was created, bringing the total to seventeen.

It will be seen that during the period of multiplication a number of Provinces had been created, covering the whole territory. Within these divisions the first need was for peace and the establishment of authority. The policy of indirect rule through the indigenous chiefs, particularly the Fulani Emirs, meant that the Provinces were closely identified with the former indigenous states. With the exception of Upper and Lower Benue the Provinces were named after emirates such as Sokoto, or independent kingdoms such as Borgu and Bornu.

The fact that 1904 marked the beginning of the period of integration demonstrates how quickly the Government faced the problems of administrative convenience and economy. It was hoped to reorganize the seventeen Provinces into eight. Seven would be formed by the amalgamation of two Provinces, and the eighth by the union of Ilorin, Kabba and Nupe Provinces. In 1904 three of the new double-Provinces were organized. Sokoto and Gando, Kano and Katagum and East and West Bornu were joined to form larger Provinces (Table 1). Table 1 shows that there were marked variations in the area and population of the various Provinces, and serves to underline the extensive use of indigenous divisions in constructing the Provincial framework.

Province	Area (sq miles)	Population (000's)
Bornu East and West	33,000	1,105
Kano	31,000	2,192
Sokoto	35,000	521
Zaria	22,000	230
Bauchi	23,200	920
Yola	16,000	290
Muri	25,800	825
Nassarawa	18,000	1,500
Nupe	6,400	150
Ilorin	6,300	255
Kabba	7,800	68
Kontagora	14,500	79
Borgu	12,000	25
Bassa	7,000	100

THE PROVINCES OF NORTHERN NIGERIA 1905 (from *Colonial Reports, Northern Nigeria*, 1905, Cmd. 3285, 1907, No. 516)

However, while Government reports continued to discuss the need to reduce further the number of Provinces, no progress was made until 1908, when Borgu Province was added to Kontagora. This was the last major reorganization before the amalgamation of the Northern and Southern Protectorates in 1914 to form the Colony and Protectorate of Nigeria. The period from 1908 to 1914 was characterized by boundary adjustments designed to avoid the division of ethnic groups and to exchange some of the geometric boundaries for lines related to the cultural and physical landscapes, which could be more easily recognized. There were twenty-one boundary changes between 1908–14; sixteen were made on ethnic grounds and five were made on grounds of accessibility or easier boundary definition, usually by a river (Fig. 5). (Letters used in the following description refer to the ethnic boundary changes; numbers refer to changes connected with accessibility or easier definition.)

The boundary of Kontagora was considerably altered on ethnic grounds. In the north-west (A) an area of 3,725 square miles was transferred to Sokoto Province. Most of this land lay west of the Niger and was inhabited by Fulani and Dandowa groups who had little in common with the Bariba of Borgu District. The region in fact corresponds closely with the area around Gombe which was held by Gando against Borgu. The smaller area of Besse, east of the river, was also inhabited mainly by Fulani. In the north-east (B) the area of Kwiambana which had formerly been part of the Emirate was added to Sokoto Province. In the south of Kontagora two small regions (C and D) around Bajibo and Takum, both occupied by members of the Nupe tribe, were transferred to Niger Province (formerly Bida or Nupe). Nineteen thousand and twenty-five square miles of the Gwari District of Zaria Province were added to Niger Province (E); this was the largest transfer made during this period of adjustment. There is no doubt that the southern portions of the transferred area were inhabited by Nupe people and that other parts were occupied by the Bassa and Ungwe groups who are more closely related, historically and culturally, to the Nupe than to the Zaria Emirate. However, there was little justification for including the Gwari people, who live in the north of the area, within Niger Province. These people are oriented towards the north, especially Katsina. It may be that this area was included to fix the boundary along the River Kara. The Koton Karifi District of Nassarawa was added to Niger Province by causing the boundary to diverge from the River Gwara (F). The Igbirra people of this valley had formerly been divided by the boundary.

From eastern Sokoto (G), 3,880 square miles were transferred to Kano Province on the dual grounds of historical association and easier administration. The new boundary lay within the former uninhabited frontier between the Katsina and Sokoto Emirates. In the east Kano also received 495 square miles of Bornu Province around Kakuri (H), which had traditionally been part of the Hadeija kingdom. This gain was offset by the transfer of 1,675 square miles of Kano Province to Bornu, east of Katagum (J). By fixing the Provincial boundary along the River Katagum it was ensured that the Bedde pagans were all reunited in Bornu Province.

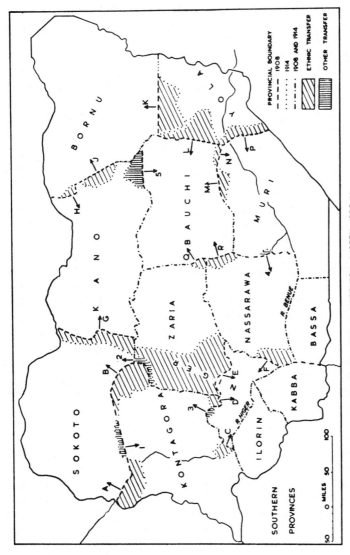

FIG. 5 PROVINCIAL BOUNDARY CHANGES IN NORTHERN NIGERIA 1908-14

Four areas were transferred to Bauchi Province for ethnic reasons. In the Bukuru area (Q and R) the boundary was moved westwards to reunite the Rukaba, Kibyen and Surawa groups. The Burranawa and Angassawa groups which had formerly been divided by the boundary between Bauchi and Muri were reunited in Bauchi Province (M). In the east of Bauchi 5,280 square miles of Yola Province were added. This area contained groups of Jerawa and Waje who were closely related to other tribes in Bauchi Province, and groups of Tula, Balawa and Terawa who had formerly been split by the Provincial boundary (L).

Muri Province was increased by transfers from Bauchi (N) and Yola (P) which reunited the Wirkum and Mumuye groups respectively. Yola was further reduced by the transfer of 6,000 square miles to Bornu Province (K). Tera, Bahur and Birra pagans occupied this area, which was marshy and which had formed part of the former frontier between Bornu and Yola.

The five changes made for reasons of accessibility or clearer boundary definition were much smaller than most of the ethnic transfers. The area of Kontagora Province was slightly increased by a northward extension to the Gulbin Ka (1) and a southward extension to the River Eba (3). Instead of just adding the Kwiambana District to Sokoto (B) the boundary was moved further south to the River Gulbi (2). There was a minor extension of Nassarawa Province at the expense of Muri when the boundary was moved eastwards to follow a short section of the Ankwe River (4). Finally, 2,625 square miles of Kano Province were transferred to Bauchi, by fixing the boundary along the River Wilka, because the transferred section could be more easily administered from Bauchi.

By 1914, when the Northern and Southern Protectorates were amalgamated, the number of Provinces had been reduced from seventeen to thirteen and extensive adjustments had been made to avoid dividing tribal groups, or groups having a common history or culture. The opportunity was taken in 1914 to make a further reduction in the number of Northern Provinces and to change some of the boundaries. Ilorin and Kabba Provinces were merged and Bassa, Muri and Nassarawa Provinces were reorganized. The meridional boundary between Bassa and Muri was moved eastwards to nine degrees East, transferring the Marchaba and Kararaba Tiv groups to Bassa Province, which was renamed Munshi Province, the capital of which was Ankpa. There is no clear reason why this change occurred since the new boundary passed through a heavily populated Tiv region. In all, about 1,400 square miles, including the important Benue station of Abinsi, were transferred to Munshi Province. North of the Benue, Muri Province was extended by the addition of Munshi District of Nassarawa Province which comprised 810 square miles. This transfer was made because the area was more accessible from the capital of Muri Province, but it is difficult to understand why the Tiv on both sides of the River Benue were not included within one Province. Formerly they were split between Muri and Nassarawa Provinces; after the reorganization they were divided between Munshi and Muri Provinces. Finally, Koton Karifi was transferred back to Nassarawa Province from Niger, re-establishing the boundary along the River Garara.

No boundary changes were made during World War I, although Yola and Bornu Provinces were increased by the inclusion of portions of the Northern Cameroons Mandated Territory. The next revision of the provincial boundaries was undertaken in 1926, and this revision provides the basis of the present Provincial structure of Northern Nigeria. As a result of the reorganization the number of Provinces was reduced to eleven by a series of boundary changes which are recorded in Fig. 6.

Kontagora was absorbed by the surrounding Provinces. Borgu was transferred to Ilorin except for an area north of Bussa which was transferred to Sokoto Province on grounds of accessibility. Sokoto Province also absorbed 8,750 square miles of northern Kontagora, which was occupied by the Rundawa and Dakakeri tribes. The remainder of Kontagora was included as a District within Niger Province. Niger Province was further increased by the inclusion of Abuja District of Nassarawa, which was largely peopled by members of the Gwari tribe. The Kwangoma and Gwari Districts of Northern Niger Province were transferred to Zaria. Zaria Province was also increased by the addition of Katsina Emirate from Kano Province. It was noted in the 1932 Provincial Report that administrative convenience alone led to the inclusion of

Katsina, Zaria and Gwari areas within one Province. While there were historical ties between Birnin Gwari and Katsina, there were no ties between these two areas and the Zaria Emirate. It seems likely that this change was partly to reduce the population preponderance of Kano Province, which was further reduced by the transfer of Katagum to Bauchi Province. Bauchi's gain in the north, however, was offset by small transfers to Bornu and large transfers of territory to the new Plateau Province. The Gwani area east of the Gongola was added to Bornu when that river became the provincial boundary. Southern Bauchi about Pankshin and Jos, together with the Amur District of north-eastern Nassarawa, formed the new Plateau Province.

Yola Province was greatly enlarged by the addition of Muri Emirate as well as the Kentu area of the Southern Provinces, when the latitudinal boundary was exchanged for the River Donga. The reasons for this change are indicated in the 1926 Report:

> It was unfortunate though inevitable, that the post-war settlement was unable to reconstitute the ancient state of Adamawa as it had been before the European division of Africa. Under the rearrangement of Provinces . . . what is possible along these lines has been done. The Province of Adamawa as now constituted comprises the whole of the former Yola Province with those parts of Adamawa which fall in the mandated territory, the Muri Emirate of the former Muri Province and the Kentu District of the mandated Cameroons Province from the Southern Provinces. (Annual Report *et seq.*, 1927, p. 6)

This quotation demonstrates first that ethnology and history still occupied the minds of the Government, and second, that there was still a mistaken impression about the extent of Adamawa. There are no historical grounds whatsoever for including Muri Emirate in Adamawa Province.

The remaining part of Muri Province was added to the remainder of Nassarawa Province and the Ankpa Division of Munshi Province to form the new Benue Province. This amalgamation had the advantage of including all the Tiv tribe in one Province. The 1926 Report suggests that the River Benue was a unifying element, and an unfortunate choice for a boundary in the earlier period. While

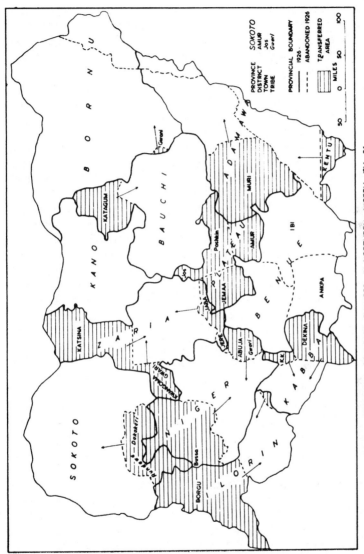

FIG. 6   PROVINCIAL BOUNDARY CHANGES IN NORTHERN NIGERIA 1914 - 26

the Benue did not divide the Tiv groups on both banks it had formed the frontier between the Nassarawa and Keffi Emirates to the north and the Aguta peoples in the south, being most effective at times of flood. The Dekina District of Munshi Province and the Koton Karifi District of Nassarawa were added to the reconstituted Kabba Province which now contained the Niger-Benue confluence. The new boundary between Ilorin and Kabba Provinces was drawn further east so that all the Nupe on the south bank were included in Lafiagi Division of Ilorin Province.

Since 1926 there have been several minor boundary changes and the formation of one new Province – Katsina. These boundary changes can be considered in two sections: those which took place in the decade after 1926 and those which occurred after 1936. This division has been adopted because 1936 was the date of publication of the only description of the boundaries of the Northern Provinces. In 1933 the Kentu Division of Adamawa was transferred to Benue. This triangular area was remote from Yola but readily accessible via the Donga valley to Wukari, one of the divisional centres of Benue Province. In the same year the Koriga area of Niger Province was added to Zaria Emirate. The Koriga area was occupied by Moslems who had indicated their wish to join Zaria. In 1934 Katsina Division of Zaria Province was created a separate Province and acquired the small Daura Emirate from Kano. Thus the amalgamation of Katsina, Gwari and Zaria was dissolved when it was clear that Katsina could be more conveniently administered separately. Gwari, despite its clear ties with Katsina, remained as part of Zaria. Also in 1934 there were three small boundary changes. The independent districts of Juba, Matoa and Kagero were subtracted from Plateau Province and added to Zaria, because both areas were occupied by one tribe. Further north the Kaje tribe was reunited in Zaria after having been divided between Zaria and Plateau Provinces. Finally, the Ilorin-Kabba boundary was extended westwards to include all the Yagba group within Kabba.

It is possible to distinguish four means of boundary definition in the description published in 1936 – by course and distance, by rivers, by relief features and by village and farm boundaries. The most common method of boundary definition is by a combination of courses and distances and turning points.

> Thence for approximately 6½ miles in a west-south-west direction passing on the south side in the Dutsin Pangur, and for approximately 2 miles in a westerly direction to cairn E34 situated on the top of Dutsin Kukuruk: thence for approximately 3½ miles in a south-west direction to cairn E33: thence for approximately 3 miles in a south-south-west direction to cairn E22 and for approximately 2¾ miles in a S.S.W. direction and for approximately 1½ miles in a W.N.W. direction to cairn E31 situated near the old side (site?) of Bagiel village.
>
> *(Nigerian Gazette*, 1936, p. 591)

This description of part of the eastern boundary of Plateau Province indicates how inexact the definition by course and distance can be: fortunately, the simple administrative functions of the boundary have not made closer definition necessary.

Many terms are used in referring to rivers as boundaries – median line, right bank, left bank, and the thalweg of the stream bed. Generally the rivers are so small that closer definition is unnecessary. However, greater precision should have been used to define the boundary through a marsh in Southern Sokoto:

> Thence along the Baduru river in a north-west direction for approximately three miles to a point where the river Baduru becomes known as the Risoko marsh; then along the marsh in a south-west direction to the Dutsin Diriri: thence in a north-west direction for approximately 15 miles to the river Dan Zaki.   *(Nigerian Gazette*, 1936, p. 593)

This section of the boundary would be most difficult to find, and disputes are much more likely to occur in areas which might be used for dry season cropping or pasture.

Hill features and village lands are each used three times in the boundary definitions. In the southern boundary of Bornu one section follows 'the range of hills bordering the Hawal valley'; between Benue and Yola Provinces part of the boundary coincides with the 'foot of the Guraji hills'; while in southern Sokoto the boundary follows the 'water-shed of the Barra Hills southwards for approximately 5 miles'. The slight use of such features indicates the low relief which is encountered throughout the area outside the British Cameroons. Isolated inselbergs were the most prominent features, and occasional boundary cairns were sited on them. Two short sections of the Zaria Provincial boundary and one section of the eastern Katsina boundary were defined by reference to village lands. One quotation from the Katsina description will illustrate the general form of this definition.

> ... thence 3¾ miles in a north-west direction to a point ½ mile north of Shodamai leaving the hamlet of Tsava to the west, thence 9 miles in a westerly direction to a point one mile south of Gazari leaving the hamlets of Durbe and Birji to the south and the hamlet of Dan Dankarsani to the north.   (*Nigerian Gazette*, 1936, p. 588)

There has been no systematic demarcation of the boundary, although some cairns and pillars have been erected by local officers, and occasional reference is made in the description to blazed trees. Some notices have been erected where boundaries intersect main roads.

Since 1936 there have been four boundary changes. In 1937 thirteen small hamlets of the Tigar and Ndoro tribes occupying an area in southern Gashaka were transferred to Benue Province on the ground of their tribal affinity with larger groups in the Kentu area. The area between the Wase and Yuli Rivers in north-west Adamawa was transferred to Plateau Province in 1948. Also in 1948 Kabba Province was enlarged by the addition of the Okpo area of south-west Benue. This transfer reunited the Igala groups which had formerly been divided. The last boundary change involved the northward movement of the boundary of Niger Province to its former position on the Gulbin Ka. This change did not eliminate the southern extension of Sokoto Province in the Niger valley to the area of Yelwa and Ngaski, which was based on the historical association of the area with the Gando Emirate.

To facilitate the policy of indirect rule, which rested on the indigenous political systems, the Provinces often had a considerable measure of ethnic homogeneity. Where tribes in adjacent Provinces employ different techniques of cultivation and house construction, the boundary coincides with clear changes in the cultural landscape.

The boundary perpetuates these landscape differences since there is little desire to move across the boundary and be part of a minority in another Province. Since most of the tribes express their tribal loyalty through a single political party, it follows that some of the Provincial boundaries mark the limits of areas of party preponderance. Further, if new Regions are created, the lines of cleavage are likely to coincide with Provincial boundaries.

The study of the evolution of Northern Nigeria's Provincial boundaries has the twin advantages that the boundaries evolved in a recent historical period and were planned as a whole, with the aim of preserving tribal homogeneity and the indigenous political structure, as far as was compatible with administrative security and efficiency. It would be much more difficult to study the evolution of the internal boundaries of England, since they developed over a much longer period and were not planned as a whole until comparatively recently.

The following section considers the interest of geographers in the planning of internal boundaries and there can be no doubt that a study of the evolution of the existing administrative boundaries is essential before any further changes are made. Without such a study it is possible that new boundaries may in fact be a regression to a former line which proved unsatisfactory in the past. There is no reason why a study of internal boundary permanence should not be rewarding to workers concerned with regional political geography, although again it must be pointed out that accurate information on the duration of internal boundaries may be difficult to acquire.

The planning of administrative areas

At various times geographers have expressed interest in the reorganization of existing local government areas. This interest is focused on the local government area rather than the boundary, an attitude which Fesler (1949) noted:

> . . . it will be well to recognize that the *boundaries* of most types of (administrative) areas are largely artificial, while the hearts of areas are real. (Fesler, 1949, p.4)

These studies are considered here because many of them prepared principles to guide internal boundary delimitation. Studies dealing with the rorganization of local government areas in England and Wales will be considered, but many other studies exist referring to other countries. No studies have been found which examine the need for the reorganization of federal boundaries, which we have noted tend to be inviolate once they are fixed. There seems to be scope for geographical analysis *before* federations are formed from unitary states, a development which occurred in Yugoslavia, Nigeria and the Colony and Protectorate of Kenya, and which may be repeated in the former Belgian Congo. However, it should be noted that in Australia, Holmes has called for the construction of planning regions which transcend federal boundaries in areas where these boundaries interfere with the integrated development of some resource, such as the Murray River valley, which is divided amongst Victoria, South Australia and New South Wales (Holmes, 1944a, 1944b, 1948). In Nigeria the Niger Delta, which is divided between the Eastern and Mid-West Regions, presents problems of administration and development because of its swampy nature and the covering of dense tropical rain forest. In an effort to overcome these problems the Delta has been constituted into a Special Area. This Special Area will still be divided between the Eastern and Mid-West Regions, but its economic advancement is the responsibility of a joint planning committee composed of federal and regional representatives.

In England and Wales, interest in the reorganization of administrative boundaries seems to have been associated with wars and the immediate post-war periods. Fawcett (1917 and 1919), Gilbert (1939) and Taylor (1942) were concerned with the delimitation of the major administrative units of England and Wales, and in 1948 Gilbert examined the need to redraw the boundaries of smaller local government areas. These writers agreed that the local government areas needed revising because they were out of date, and did not meet the requirements of the local authorities, many of which had been transformed in population, size and economic importance since the boundaries were drawn. There were many criticisms of the boundaries. First, it was claimed that they were inefficient and inconvenient, because they were drawn to serve different functions and were not coincident. Second, the frequent separation of urban and rural areas, and places of occupation and residence, were judged to be inimicable to the integrated development of the regions. Third, the growing conurbations in England, which required a uniform development plan, were split between two or more administrations. Fourth, there was the complaint that in many cases the boundaries ignored local sentiments and divided groups who were conscious of a community spirit. A concensus of these four papers indicated that the boundary reorganization should be guided by the following principles:

1. All government areas should be composed of aggregates of the smallest basic unit, in such a way that the boundaries were multifunctional.

2. As far as possible each main administrative area should include related urban and rural areas, and residential and industrial districts.

3. Conurbations should be constituted into single administrative areas, capable of co-ordinating development.

4. Fawcett was alone in recommending that boundaries should be drawn through lightly populated or uninhabited areas, and should follow watersheds, to avoid unnecessary divisions of water, road and sewage services, which generally follow valleys.

5. The boundary should be drawn to cater for local sentiment and regional patriotism.

Clearly the application of the first four principles would indicate the general border zone between administrative units, while the last would provide information for the detailed siting of the boundary within that zone. It was probably for this reason that Gilbert (1948) called for research into social geography 'in the proper meaning of that misused term'. Unfortunately it is not generally appreciated that local sentiment is one of the strongest forces opposing boundary revision, because the ability of internal boundaries to influence the development of the cultural landscape and the attitudes of its inhabitants is underrated. To illustrate this point we can use the experience of the Local Government Commission for England, which was authorized by the Local Government Act (1958) to review local government boundaries and recommend changes to produce more convenient and efficient administration. The Commission's findings for various parts of the country have been published, and in all cases they have provoked a storm of protest from local representatives. When the proposed boundary changes for Somerset were published it was complained that they would 'extinguish seven distinct, historic entities, some of them dating back to Domesday' (*The Times*, London, November 14th, 1961). The proposal to transfer Lyme Regis to Devon from Dorset was resisted by the local inhabitants 'supported by traditions of many centuries, binding the people of Lyme Regis to the County of Dorset' (*The Times*, London, December 21st, 1961). It has not even proved possible to find common support for the unification of the administration of conurbations, although such a step seems desirable. The proposal to replace seventeen authorities by four County Boroughs, which together would form the County of Tyneside, is opposed by several of the authorities, which are anxious to preserve their identity. Boldon Urban District regards itself as a green belt and dormitory between the populous areas of Tyneside and Sunderland, and resists inclusion within either. The authorities threatened with partition to the north of Tyneside also resist the proposal.

Whether the solution to the problems of out-of-date internal boundaries is sought in new boundaries, or in the change of boundary functions and the development of special relationships between contiguous administrative units, the geographer has a contribution to make. This main contribution lies in the collection of information, based on detailed research, which includes a record of the boundary evolution, and an understanding of the way in which internal boundaries influence the development of the landscape and personal attitudes. Until this body of knowledge is available there is no guarantee that new internal boundaries will be notably more successful than their predecessors.

Federal boundary disputes

While there appear to be no studies of internal boundary disputes, several writers have considered federal boundary disputes. These writers include lawyers, historians and geographers, and it is interesting to compare their various approaches. Lawyers are generally concerned with the manner in which each claimant prosecutes his case before the local and federal law courts, the legal arguments on precedent and the admissibility of evidence, the interpretation of the boundary definition, and the formal decision of the court. Historians are generally concerned with the evolution of the dispute and the economic and social factors which have encouraged it to assume greater or less significance at various times. There is also an attempt by historians to assess the role of the main personalities concerned in the dispute, and the extent to which they were influenced by contemporary events and philosophical concepts. The geographer finds some common ground with both lawyers and historians. Like the lawyer, the geographer is interested in interpreting the boundary definition in the light of contemporary maps and geographical knowledge. On the other hand, the geographer shares the evolutionary interest of the historian, by discovering the geographical factors which have contributed to the development of the dispute. Lastly, the geographer is concerned with understanding the significance of the dispute to the economic and political development of the landscape, and in following the changes which may ensue after the dispute has been settled.

The causes of boundary disputes may be classified into three groups:

1. Ambiguous or incomplete boundary definition

2. Superimposition of the boundary upon the cultural landscape in a way which, for example, divides national or linguistic groups, hinders resource development or restricts trade

3. Significant changes in the political or economic circumstances of one or both of the states separated by the boundary.

Each of these categories will be considered in turn.

The majority of papers concerned with federal boundary disputes deal with cases which have arisen through the ambiguous or incomplete definition of the boundary; examples are taken from the United States, Australia and Nigeria. The boundaries of Texas have provided several interesting disputes which have been studied mainly by historians. Bowman (1923), Carpenter (1925), and Billington (1959) have examined the dispute between Oklahoma and Texas, where they are divided by the Red River. This dispute arose because the northern boundary of Texas was stated to be the south bank of the Red River, while the southern boundary of Oklahoma was put along the middle of the main channel. In any case Oklahoma had no rights over the bed of the river, because it was not navigable when Oklahoma was admitted to the Union; these rights belonged to the Federal Government. For a time the non-coincidence of the two boundaries was a merely academic matter, but this was changed when oil was discovered along the south bank. Immediately there was a flood of prospectors, and licences were granted by Texas, Oklahoma and the Federal Government. The dispute was further complicated by the frequent accretionary changes of the Red River, and the presence of an Indian Reservation in the Oklahoma border area.

Bowden's interesting study (1959) of the Texas-New Mexico boundary dispute explains why the present boundary follows the course of the Rio Grande as it was on September 9th, 1850, although the final legal decision was not settled until 1913. Chapman's paper (1949) on the Texan claim to Greer County reviews the historical development of the dispute and considers in some detail the survey and demarcation of the resulting boundary. The dispute, related to the Sabine River where it divides Texas and Louisiana, has similar features to the Red River dispute, since it arises because of the non-coincidence of the eastern Texas boundary and the western Louisiana boundary, leaving a neutral strip of territory seventy miles long by 150 feet wide (Andrew, 1949).

Six papers consider in detail the problems associated with the interpretation of boundary definitions. In 1930, Martin recorded in detail the arguments used in the Michigan-Wisconsin boundary dispute from 1923–1936, and the final judgement. The dispute arose through claims by Michigan to territory administered by Wisconsin, and the matter turned on the interpretation of such terms as 'the most usual ship channel', and the identification of the Lake of the Desert with either Island Lake (claimed by Michigan) or Lac Vieux Desert (claimed by Wisconsin). As a result of an error made in defining the adjudicated boundary in 1926, a further case was brought between 1932–36, and this was also described in detail by Martin.

Ogier examined the Victoria State claim to a boundary along the

Murrumbidgee River instead of the Murray River, in three papers published between 1902–12. The whole case turned on the interpretation of the phrase 'a straight line drawn from Cape Howe to the nearest source of the River Murray'. Ogier contends that the source of the Murrumbidgee is also a source of the River Murray, and closer to Cape Howe than the source of the Hume River, another Murray tributary. Although the argument seems geographically impeccable, the River Hume continues to mark the federal boundary.

Prescott (1959) considered the unsatisfactory nature of the definition of Nigeria's federal boundaries, and suggested that considerable problems of interpretation may have to be faced in the future.

Boundary disputes arising through the superimposition of the boundary on a cultural landscape, or the change in economic and political conditions since the boundary was drawn, may be treated together. Two examples are considered by Holdegel (1959) and Prescott (1959). Holdegel reviewed the problems resulting from the creation of the Federal State of Baden-Württemburg, with boundaries which divided areas of similar local and regional loyalties. He stresses the lasting importance of historical associations in these areas, and regrets the divisions between towns such as Hirsch (Essen) and Heidelberg (Baden-Württemburg), and between Ulm (Baden-Württemburg), and Neu-Ulm (Bavaria). It would have been interesting if Holdegel had been able to define more closely the regions of community consciousness, and indicate to what extent there were conflicts between the local and regional attachments. Holdegel calls for a *natürliche Grenze* along the crest of the Oldenwald but does not explain why such a boundary would be more satisfactory.

The ethnic disputes associated with Nigeria's federal boundaries result from political developments since the boundaries were delimited. It has already been explained (see p. 154) that the present federal boundaries were delimited before 1939. The division of such tribal groups as the Yoruba, Ibo, and Ijaw could be explained by the fact that the two Yoruba factions had been at war with each other when the original boundary was drawn in 1894, and because the Ibo and Ijaw tribes had no coherent political structure, political development having been restricted to the family or clan level. Since 1939 two important developments have taken place. First, the traditional tribal loyalties have been transferred to tribal political parties, which have given a measure of unity to the Ibo and Ijaw. These parties have focused attention on the lack of coincidence between the federal boundaries and the *new* ethnic-political patterns. Second, the situation has been exacerbated by the increased functions assumed by the federal boundaries since 1959.

This brief review suggests that federal boundary disputes caused by ambiguous or incomplete definition may occur in all federations. Disputes resulting from the superimposition of the boundary upon elements of the cultural landscape are likely to occur only when a new federal state is created, as in Germany, or when powerful, national-tribal loyalties exist, as in the African federations. The absence of reference to internal boundary disputes is not conclusive evidence that none exists. The outcry by certain sections against the proposed reorganization of British local government areas suggest that some disputes may exist, but it may well be that such disputes are considered too parochial for study.

Conclusion

This chapter has discussed the significant differences between international and intra-national boundaries, and suggests that intra-national boundaries can be divided into two distinct groups – federal and internal. A review of the literature concerned with the geographical aspects of intra-national boundaries reveals that federal boundaries have been more frequently considered than internal boundaries. There is a close similarity of subject and method between intra-national and international boundary studies, although internal boundaries have one unique facet related to their planning.

It seems worthwhile to outline the main aspects of intra-national boundaries to which geographers might address themselves in future.

There is great need to develop a classification of internal boundaries which will facilitate the correlation of different studies and allow clarification of ideas related to internal boundaries. Fesler (1949) has suggested a primary division between *governmental boundaries*, enclosing areas with a measure of functional or fiscal autonomy, and *field service boundaries*, which delimit areas lacking any functional or fiscal autonomy, but which are drawn for the convenient execution of individual government departments. Geographers may find this a useful starting point, but they will also have to consider non-governmental boundaries used by private companies and organizations in order to understand their significance.

The political geographer can make a useful contribution to the planning of internal boundaries, mainly in respect of position, but to a lesser extent in terms of function. More studies of the evolution of internal boundaries, their impact on the cultural landscape and local boundary disputes, would do much to provide a firm foundation on which subsequent boundary changes could be made. Techniques for such studies bear close relationships to those used in connexion with international boundaries. However, it is to be hoped that the precise statistical data, associated with internal boundaries, will make it possible to develop more exact methods for their analysis. Studies of the kind envisaged would be useful to both long-established and recently independent states. In both cases the revision of boundaries, in the light of detailed research, could result in increased efficiency and economy. In some of the former colonial territories, which have recently been granted independence, the redesigned internal boundaries could contribute to the state's political unity. In Nigeria and in other British colonies the internal boundaries were drawn to preserve tribal structures, through which the policy of indirect rule could be applied. The continuation of such boundaries will perpetuate tribal consciousness and create problems for the new administration. However, the colonial boundaries are in many cases deeply intrenched into the cultural and political fabric of the state, and their revision may evoke considerable opposition.

References

ANDREW, B. H., 1949, 'Some queries concerning the Texas-Louisiana Sabine boundary', *Southwestern Historical Quart.*, 53, pp. 1–18.
BILLINGTON M., 1959, 'The Red River boundary controversy', ibid., 62, pp. 356–63.

BOWDEN, J. J., 1959, 'The Texas-New Mexico boundary dispute along the Rio Grande', ibid., 63. pp. 221–37.

BOWMAN, I., 1923, 'An American boundary dispute; decision of the Supreme Court with respect to the Texas-Oklahoma boundary', *Geogr. Rev.*, 13, pp. 161–81.

CARPENTER, W. C., 1925. 'The Red River boundary dispute', *Am. Journ. International Law*, 19, pp. 517–29.

CHAPMAN, B. B., 1949, 'The claims of Texas to Greer County', *Southwestern Historical Quart.*, 53, pp. 401–24.

DAY, W. M., 1949, 'The relative permanence of former boundaries in India', *Scottish Geographical Magazine*, 65, pp. 113–22.

DEUTSCH, H. J., 1960, 'The evolution of state and territorial boundaries in the Inland Empire of the Pacific Northwest', *Pacific Northwestern Quart.*, 51, pp. 115–31.

FAWCETT, C. B., 1917, 'Natural divisions of England', *Geogr. J.*, 49, pp. 124–41.

FAWCETT, C. B., 1919, new ed. 1960, East, W. G., and Wooldridge, S. W. (Eds.), *Provinces of England*, London.

FENELON, P., 1956, 'Structure géographique et frontières des Départements français', *Abstract of Papers*, 18th International Geographical Congress, Rio de Janeiro, p. 186.

FESLER, J. W., 1949, *Area and Administration*, Alabama.

GILBERT, E. W., 1939, 'Practical regionalism in England and Wales', *Geogr. J.*, 94, pp. 24–44.

GILBERT, E. W., 1948, 'The boundaries of local government areas', *Geogr. J.*, 111, pp. 172–206.

GRISWOLD, E. N., 1939, 'Hunting boundaries with car and camera, in the northeastern United States', *Geogr. Rev.*, 29, pp. 353–82.

HARTSHORNE, R., 1933, 'Geographic and political boundaries in Upper Silesia', *Annals*, Association of American Geographers, 23, pp. 195–228.

HARTSHORNE, R., 1950, 'The Franco-German boundary of 1871', *World Politics*, 2, pp. 209–50.

HOLDEGEL, H., 1959, 'Grenzproblem des Südwest Staates', *Zeitschrift für Geopolitik*, 30, pp. 9–19.

HOLMES, J. M., 1944a, *The geographical basis of planning*, Sydney.

HOLMES, J. M., 1944b, 'Regional boundaries in the Murray valley.' *Australian Geographer*, 4, pp. 197–203.

HOLMES, J. M., 1948, 'Regional planning in Australia', *Geogr. J.*, 112, pp. 78–82.

HOUSE, J. W., 1959, 'The Franco-Italian boundary in the Alpes Maritimes', *Transactions*, Institute of British Geographers, 26, pp. 107–31.

JONES, S. B., 1945, *Boundary Making*, Carnegie Endowment for International Peace, Division of International Law, No. 8, Washington.

MACKAY, J. R., 1960, 'The interactance hypothesis and boundaries in Canada – a preliminary study', *Canadian Geographer*, 16, pp. 1–8.

MARTIN, L., 1930, 'The Michigan-Wisconsin boundary case in the Supreme Court of the United States', *Annals*, Association of American Geographers, 20, pp. 105–63.

MARTIN, L., 1938, 'The second Wisconsin-Michigan boundary case in the Supreme Court of the United States', *Annals*, Association of American Geographers, 28, pp. 77–126.

MORRISON, J. A., 1938, 'The evolution of the territorial-administrative system of the U.S.S.R.', *Amer. Quart. on the Soviet Union*, 1, pp. 25–46.

NELSON, H. J., 1952, 'The Vernon area of California – a study of the political factor in urban geography', *Annals*, Association of American Geographers, 42, pp. 177–91.

NICHOLSON, N. L., 1954, *The boundaries of Canada, its Provinces and Territories*, Department of Mines and Technical Survey, Geographical Branch, Memoir 2, Ottawa.

OGIER, J. C. H., 1902, 'The question of the original official boundary between the States of New South Wales and Victoria', *Victorian Geographical Journ.*, 20 (New series), 71–84.

OGIER, J. C. H., 1905, 'The Victorian State boundary', ibid., 23, pp. 78–106.

OGIER, J. C. H., 1912, 'The Riverina', ibid., 29, pp. 49–85.

PAULLIN, C. O., 1932, *Atlas of the historical geography of the United States*, New York, pp. 72–87.

PRESCOTT, J. R. V., 1959a, 'The evolution of Nigeria's boundaries' *Nigerian Geographical Journ.*, 2, pp. 80–104.

PRESCOTT, J. R. V., 1959b, 'Nigeria's regional boundary problems', *Geogr. Rev.*, 49, pp. 485–505.

Report on the Amalgamation of Northern and Southern Nigeria and their administration, Cmd. 468, H.M.S.O., 1920, p. 11.

ROSE, A. J., 1955, 'The border between Queensland and New South Wales', *Australian Geographer*, 6, pp. 3–18.,

SHABAD, T., 1956, 'The administrative-territorial patterns of the Soviet Union', Chapter 15 in East, W. G., and Moodie A. E. (Eds.), *The changing world*, London.

SPATE, O. H. K., 1957, *India and Pakistan*, London.

TAYLOR, E. G. R., 1942, 'Discussion on the geographical aspects of regional planning', *Geogr. J.*, 99, pp. 61–80.

THOMAS, B. E., 1949, 'Demarcation of the boundaries of Idaho', *Pacific Northwest Quart.*, 40, pp. 24–34.

ULLMAN, E. L., 1938, 'Political geography in the Pacific Northwest', *Scottish Geographical Magazine*, 54, pp. 236–9.

ULLMAN, E. L., 1939, 'The eastern Rhode Island-Massachusetts boundary zone', *Geogr. Rev.*, 29, pp. 291–302.

WATSON, J. W., 1948, 'The influence of the frontier on Niagara settlements', *Geogr. Rev.*, 38, pp. 113–19.

WHITTLESEY, D., 1956, 'The United States', Chapters 9 and 10 in East, W. G., and Moodie, A. E. (Eds.), *The changing world*, London.

WISKEMANN, E., 1956, *Germany's eastern neighbours*, London.

YONEKURA, J., 1956, 'Historical development of the political-administrative divisions of Japan', *Abstract of Papers*, 18th International Geographical Congress, Rio de Janeiro.

Index